Children with Acquired Aphasias

Janet A. Lees

MPhil, DipCST, RegMCSLT, Cert Theol (Oxon)

Honorary Consultant Speech and Language Therapist
Wolfson Child Development Centre,
The Hospitals for Sick Children, Great Ormond Street, London
Adviser to The College of Speech and Language Therapists, London

Foreword by

Brian Neville, FRCP

Professor of Paediatric Neurology, Institute of Child Health,
Honorary Consultant Paediatric Neurologist,
The Hospitals for Sick Children, Great Ormond Street, London

Whurr Publishers Ltd
London

© 1993 Whurr Publishers Ltd

First published 1993 by
Whurr Publishers Ltd
19B Compton Terrace, London N1 2UN, England
Published and distributed in the USA and Canada by
SINGULAR PUBLISHING GROUP, INC.
4284 41st Street
San Diego, California 92105

British Library Cataloguing-in-Publication Data
A catalogue record for this book is available from the
British Library.

ISBN 1-870332-69-5

Library of Congress Cataloging-in-Publication Data
A catalogue record for this book is available.
Singular no.: 1-565932-52-8

Photoset by Computape (Pickering) Ltd, North Yorkshire
Printed and bound in the UK by Athenaeum Press Ltd, Newcastle upon Tyne

Foreword

It is a great pleasure to introduce this clinical study, which reviews a therapist's experience of 'acquired aphasias in childhood'. Detailed case studies of the type presented in this book are a valid contribution to science at the stage at which the framework for the study of the subject is unclear. Attempts at more fundamental studies tend to run into problems of classification and an uneven or incomplete pattern of investigation, both neurological and cognitive. Any general theory has to recognise that the phenotype presented in each case did exist and requires explanation. A good source of testable hypotheses in the area of childhood aphasia is therefore well-documented clinical experience.

The purposes of classification of a medical problem and of its study require definition. A developmental disability arising from damage to the central nervous system and defined by its phenotype contains the following elements:

1. It is occurring on a moving baseline of normal development upon which further development is to be expected.
2. The assessment tools need to be appropriate for the developmental age of the child, and, in young children, this inevitably means that some functions will not be accessible.
3. Plasticity in the developing nervous system may allow the preservation of certain functions, particularly those related to language. From a theoretical standpoint, plasticity could involve relocation of function to the opposite hemisphere or elsewhere in the same hemisphere, or the accessing of a secondary, less efficient system.
4. Normal recovery is a most dramatic and unexplained phenomenon and occurs whether the person is 1 or 21 years old and should not be confused with plasticity.
5. Critical periods for the development of a particular function may exist, which, at most, cannot be retrieved. This may, for example, apply to the

v

development of social communication in young children at relatively high risk of the development of autistic features. One such situation appears to exist in young children with tuberous sclerosis early-onset epilepsy.

6. A relationship will exist with an adult model of acquired aphasia. The differences in the findings in such a model may reflect the above factors, but importantly may indicate defects in the adult model itself.

7. Any syndrome defined by the occurrence of acquired aphasia cannot, by definition, reflect the range of expression of the underlying pathologies.

These are the developmental dimensions that both enliven and complicate the study of aphasia in the paediatric age group. If we look critically at the purposes of the study of acquired aphasia in childhood, these could include the following:

1. To study the pathology of language localisation in normal and pathological situations. If this is the 'lesion model' then so be it. This methodology can now exploit the ability of modern imaging to identify lesions, and of functional imaging to demonstrate either loss, spread or relocation of areas of high metabolic rate during specific activities. Position emission tomography (PET) has limited use in childhood because the technique uses ionising radiation; however, the possibility of magnetic resonance functional imaging is a most exciting prospect.

2. To study the mechanisms of language function in the normal and pathological situations. Such research may have many starting points. It could, for example, be examining the primacy of memory or the development of symbolic understanding or be looking at the primary drive to communicate. Research in this field may arise from the construction of theoretical models or be substrate-based.

It is into this largely uncharted area that Janet Lees has written this book. Such detailed clinical studies are a valuable starting point for clinical research. They also allow therapists and doctors to develop their skills and widen their experience of this uncommon problem. This will, it is hoped, allow the children who have acute language problems and their families to feel supported and understood, even if the professionals remain uncertain as to whether the intervention programme is effective. I commend this book as an important and very useful contribution to the subject.

B. G. R. Neville

Preface

It was in 1981, while still a student at the School for the Study of Disorders of Human Communication in London, that I first became interested in acquired childhood aphasia (ACA). In our third and final year as students for the then Diploma of the College of Speech Therapists, I found the study of aphasiology fascinating but the prospect of working with aphasic adults did not appeal to me, and I have to say that I have never worked with adults. Instead, in the clinical placement of my final year I was able to work with two children who had ACA subsequent to head injuries. This is where this book began.

Part of the fascination of ACA for me was the mystery that surrounded it. Papers written in the 1940s were the first studies with this clinical group, and yet there seemed to have been little progress up to the late 1970s. I resolved to learn more and was fortunate to have the opportunity to discuss the whole matter with one of the leading aphasiologists of the day, H. Hecaen, whose 1976 paper on ACA was the most widely available at the time. Others have commented on the willingness of Professor Hecaen to discuss anything with even the newest student and, in my faltering French, I was no exception.

I had seen four children with ACA by 1984 when I began working at Guy's Hospital with Brian Neville. From then on I had the opportunity to study almost as much ACA as I could, so that a longitudinal study became a real possibility. I started this at the end of 1984, when Professor Bob Fawcus offered me a place to study for a postgraduate degree at the new Department of Clinical Communication Studies at the City University, London. The study was supervised by Dr Dorothy Bishop, then at the University of Manchester, who has researched widely in paediatric language disorder, both developmental and acquired.

Throughout the 1980s there have been many exciting and challenging developments. Because of the small numbers of children seen at any one centre, the study of ACA has gradually developed into a network, particularly across Europe. I remember particularly stimulating discussions with Hugo van Dongen, Christa Loonen, Philippe Paquier and Edgar de Wijngaert as we worked together to further our understanding of ACA.

In the introduction to my thesis I said that I had learnt much from the children I had worked with and that 'not all of that was about acquired childhood aphasia'. Human development is a fascinating area of study which benefits from the interaction of many disciplines. The speech and language therapist works best as a member of a team. Speech and language therapy is itself a discipline that combines a number of ways of thinking and working, and integrates medical, educational, psychological, linguistic and sociological models. It is the integration of these perspectives into a holistic child-centred model that is fundamental to speech and language therapy as outlined both in *Children with Language Disorders* (Lees and Urwin, 1991), in which some of my early work on ACA is discussed alongside work on developmental language problems, and in this present book.

As a speech and language therapist who is also a theologian I must also say that the study of ACA is a pilgrimage in faith: mostly exciting and fun, sometimes sad, difficult and even occasionally lonely. It is still ongoing. It did not end when I finished my thesis and I doubt that it will end with the completion of this book. In science we test hypotheses and in Christian theology we use a method of action/reflection that calls on us to examine our experiences critically in the light of scripture and the Christian tradition and, from that reflection, to take the next step in faith. These both seem to me to be methods I employ as a speech and language therapist. This book is a reflection on 10 years of study of ACA, of discussions and developments in the light of research by myself and with others. To remain true to my model the next step has to be taken in faith: the faith that the revelation continues and that ultimately we shall know and be known. As Sydney Carter has it in his hymn: 'One more step along the world I go ... and it's from the old I travel to the new.' And so do I.

Janet A. Lees
Mansfield College, Oxford
Easter 1993

Contents

Acknowledgements

There are many people who have supported my work in ACA: friends and colleagues at the Newcomen Child Development Centre, Guy's Hospital, where most of this work was carried out; many speech and language therapists throughout the country; members of the United Reformed Church in the United Kingdom, especially those congregations at Hatfield Heath, Halsted and Palmers Green; and colleagues at Mansfield College, Oxford.

I would also like to thank those members of my family who support the work I do: my husband, Bob Warwicker, for his help with editing; my father, Doug Lees, for the two illustrations, Figures 1.1 and 6.1; and my mother, Anne Lees, who was my first role-model in this ministry of healing.

List of cases

Note: the cases marked † were first described by Lees and Neville (1990) and those marked * by Lees and Urwin (1991).

Abbreviations

ACA	acquired childhood aphasia
CAST	Children's Aphasia Screening Test
CNS	central nervous system
CSF	cerebrospinal fluid
CT	computed tomography
dB	decibel
EEG	electroencephalogram
GCE	General Certificate of Education
GCS	Glasgow Coma Score
GCSE	General Certificate of Secondary Education
GNT	Graded Naming Test
Hz	hertz
IQ	intelligence quotient
kg	kilogram
MRI	magnetic resonance imaging
NMR	nuclear magnetic resonance
PET	positron emission tomography
PICAC	Porch Index of Communicative Ability in Children
RDLS	Reynell Developmental Language Scales
s.d.	standard deviation
TROG	Test for Reception of Grammar
WFVT	Word Finding Vocabulary Test
WISC(R)	Wechsler Intelligence Scale for Children (revised)
w.t.e.	whole time equivalent

Chapter 1
Introduction

The acquired aphasias of childhood are those language disorders that appear after a period of normal language development and are secondary to cerebral dysfunction. No large-scale studies of the epidemiology of acquired childhood aphasias (ACAs) have been carried out, but small-scale studies (Robinson, 1987, 1991) suggest that they are considerably rarer than developmental language impairments. Robinson (1987, 1991) reported two series which suggested that acquired aphasias accounted for between 4% and 7% of cases of language impairment in children. Yet it seems likely that, with improvements in paediatric intensive care facilities, more children will be surviving serious brain injury, one of the potential causes of ACAs. Additionally, in the long term, the statutory provision of assessment of special educational needs under the 1981 Education Act means that those surviving will need to be provided with appropriate assessment and management services. Therefore, although currently few speech and language therapists have much experience with this population, there is an increasing likelihood that they will find children with acquired aphasias under their care.

In this introductory chapter, the range of causes of ACAs will be outlined, and are dealt with in greater depth later in the book. The traditional classification of childhood aphasia into traumatic and convulsive subgroups has been followed, because the classification relates to previous research into these disorders for which no entirely satisfactory classification system has been suggested. However, this does mean that some issues relating to assessment and management will be repeated or referred to in several chapters, and this will be indicated in the text. This chapter also deals with some of the issues underlying our study and present understanding of ACA, the different neuropathologies and their consequences, the problems of assessment and management, and the question of recovery. All of these issues will be dealt with in the relevant chapters in the context of specific ACA subtypes.

1

The causes of loss or deterioration of language in childhood

Most clinicians probably view the results of severe brain injury, particularly after closed head injury, as being typical cases of ACA. However, there are many causes of loss or deterioration of language in childhood as Table 1.1 shows. Some of these causes to date have attracted more research interest than others, and previous research is dealt with in the relevant chapters.

Although children have probably been suffering from ACA in its many forms for centuries, only since about 1978 have they become the subject of significant research and clinical interest. Traditionally, researchers have divided these language problems into two broad groups: aphasias of traumatic origin, and language problems whose origin is thought to be connected to convulsions. For the sake of clarity and to provide a comprehensive account, this division has been followed in this book, Part I dealing with the traumatic aphasias and Part II with the convulsive aphasias. The traumatic subgroup includes various types of direct cerebral damage or invasion of cerebral tissue, including ischaemia, and viral and bacterial agents. On the fringe of the traumatic group, cerebral anoxia is also discussed. However, this does not suggest that so-called traumatic and convulsive aetiologies are not closely related; in fact cases in which the two aetiologies converge are also discussed. Such aetiologically anomalous aphasias are discussed in the final chapter, together with brief discussion of some of the other conditions involving the symptom of regression of language during childhood.

Some aetiologies do not fit easily into the traumatic (damage)/convulsive categorisation. Furthermore, there are those who feel that the division puts too much emphasis on the medical aspects of ACAs and that consideration of the presenting features of the language disorders would be more useful to the clinician. However, the range and types of language disorders encountered in ACA will not be overlooked, and a number of different models of the classification of language disorders and their application to ACA will be discussed. In the future, we hope that further research into language disorder subtypes presenting in ACAs will lead to the development of a more appropriate linguistic classification.

Throughout the book, the aim is to provide information and an approach that can be directly related to clinical practice. A wide range of cases will be discussed and details of assessment procedures, short- and long-term recovery, and management strategies given. The idea of this approach is to establish a basis from which the clinician can work with these children. The presentation of the cases has formed the basis of recent clinical research into ACA (Lees, 1989, 1993; Lees and Neville, 1990), and was used in the presentation of cases of children with language disorders – both developmental and acquired – in Lees and Urwin (1991). The technique can also be seen in use with the client groups of Brindley et al. (1993).

Table 1.1 Causes of loss or deterioration of language in childhood

Aphasias of traumatic origin

1. Head injury: open or closed

   Diffuse and bilateral damage may be combined with additional focal damage

   Additional problems may include motor, cognitive and sensory deficits, so influencing rehabilitation needs

   Epilepsy may be a sequel

   Where initial aphasia is very severe and persists for more than 6 months, prognosis for complete recovery is poor

   In young children later acquisition of written language may be impaired

2. Unilateral cerebrovascular lesions

   Damage is essentially focal

   Visual field defects and hemiplegia may also occur

   Epilepsy may be a sequel

   Even when initial aphasia is severe a return to within -2 s.d. for verbal comprehension score within 6 months of onset is usually indicative of a good prognosis

3. Cerebral infections

   Meningitis and encephalitis

   Usually diffuse effect and additional motor, cognitive and sensory deficits are common in severe cases

   Cerebral abscess

   Essentially a focal effect, probably to temporal or frontal lobes

   Where the damage is purely cortical, as with a subdural empyema, the aphasia is usually only moderate to mild

4. Other causes of traumtic aphasias

   Surgical removal of cerebral tumour

   Effect is usually focal

   Initial or delayed period of mutism is common

   Epilepsy may be a sequel

   Malignancy of initial tumour and effect of other treatment (radiotherapy, chemotherapy) may be additional factors in prognosis

   Cerebral anoxia

   Effect is usually difuse

   Additional problems may include motor, cognitive and sensory deficits

Table 1.1 continued

Aphasias of convulsive origin

5. Landau–Kleffner syndrome

   May be preceded or followed by epilepsy but one-third of cases never have epilepsy

   Major feature of language is a severe receptive aphasia

   Language comprehension may deteriorate over a long period. Where this shows little recovery over first 6 months the prognosis is poor

   Loss of language comprehension may be acute, sometimes in association with another illness. Where recovery is good in first 3 months (to within − 2 s.d.) prognosis is good

   Language comprehension may fluctuate in association with temporal lobe EEG abnormalities. Where this can be controlled by anticonvulsants prognosis is moderate to good

6. Other convulsive aphasias

   Aphasia may occur as a consequence of convulsive status, as a post-ictal phenomenon, or as a feature of minor epileptic status

   Other learning problems may also occur in association, particularly after long and repeated convulsive status

   Language disturbance may be fleeting, short term (less than 24 hours), more long term or fluctuating

Other syndromes in which there is a loss or deterioration of language

7. Late-onset autism

   A pervasive developmental disorder of the autistic type which is preceded by a period of normal development

   Loss of social and communication skills is the major sign. Severe receptive language disorder is common. There may be an accompanying deterioration in other cognitive skills

8. Rett's syndrome

   Developmental disorder in which communication, motor and cognitive skills are lost between 6 and 12 months of age

   All known cases are girls

   Other clinical signs include: inappropriate social interaction, slowing of head growth, severe communication difficulties, abnormal hand and oral movements

Note: adapted from Lees and Urwin (1991).

A history of the study of ACA

The modern study of aphasia can be traced back to the work of Broca (1824–1880) and Wernicke (1848–1905). As neurologists they were both responsible, at least in part, for the clear description of adults who suffered loss of language as a result of cerebral disease. The lesion-based maps of the cerebral cortex subsequently developed, which attributed certain aspects of language function to specific locations within the cerebral hemispheres, were based on such observations. A simplified version of such a map is shown in Figure 1.1

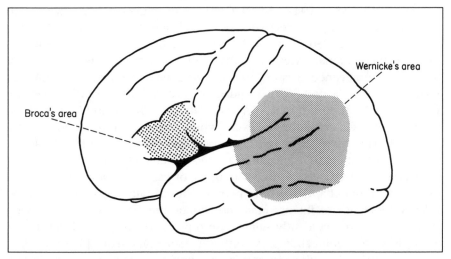

Figure 1.1 Diagrammatic representation of the left cerebral cortex showing Broca's and Wernicke's areas.

The school of thought which was developed by Broca and Wernicke continues to have a significant influence on our understanding of language breakdown in adults, although it has been recognised as having more limited application to the study of childhood language disorders, whether developmental or acquired. Although we are a long way from understanding the brain's response to injury in childhood, it is unlikely that a simple model relying solely on the position of cerebral lesions would account for all the variations that are seen. Other variables, such as age at injury, the nature, location and extent of brain injury, and the path of recovery, require consideration. As Bishop (1988) said: 'anyone attempting to assimilate the literature on acquired aphasia in children soon becomes frustrated at the paucity of the data and the lack of detail given in many of the published cases.' An outline of some of the main studies in the past quickly demonstrates some of these problems.

It was not until 1942 that there was any systematic reporting in the literature of large numbers of children presenting with ACAs. Guttman (1942) reported a series of 16 children with ACAs resulting from a range of aetiologies. His report seemed to suggest that aphasia after right hemisphere lesions was more common in children than in adults. This was later restated by Hecaen (1976). This controversy was not tackled until 1982 by Carter, Hohengger and Satz; they concluded that by excluding early studies in which the incidence of ACAs was conflictingly reported, and amalgamating the evidence from later studies, the data proved to be consistent with electrophysiological, neuroanatomical and behavioural data supporting the developmental invariance position – i.e. in most human beings the left cerebral hemisphere is dominant for language function before birth.

Similarly, between 1942 and 1976 studies of traumatic ACA emphasised the rapid and complete recovery of speech and language skills in such children. This then led to the neglect of the study of ACA by aphasiologists because the dominant view was that childhood aphasia was seldom of long-term significance (Lesser, 1978). It was also accepted that ACA was characterised by a non-fluent language disorder. Guttman (1942) set the trend when he reported that ACA was a 'motor aphasia' and he noted the absence of 'sensory aphasia' even when temporal lobe lesions were reported. This view went more or less unchallenged until 1978 when Woods and Teuber (1978) reported a series which included a 5-year-old boy with jargon aphasia. Since then a number of cases, including some small groups, with fluent aphasias have been reported. Satz (1991) reviewed the relative incidence of fluent versus non-fluent aphasias in children, noting that they are predominantly single case reports. He concluded that fluent aphasias were significantly less common than non-fluent aphasias, when compared to adult studies. He stated: 'it seems reasonable to conclude that the symptom picture in childhood aphasia is predominantly nonfluent'; using the previous three largest series he estimated that non-fluent aphasias were probably in excess of 85% of total aphasias in children.

In 1957 a type of ACA that did not appear to be related to trauma was first described by Landau and Kleffner. This puzzling syndrome has many names, the most common being 'acquired receptive aphasia with convulsive disorder' or the Landau–Kleffner syndrome (Landau and Kleffner, 1957). Researchers have now spent about 30 years trying to decide, among other things, whether it is one syndrome and what part convulsive disorder plays in the aetiology.

The main problems of the pre-1978 period were the small number of cases reported and the rather ad hoc methodology employed in the studies, making it very difficult to conduct meaningful comparisons between studies on the basis of either neurology or the language problems observed. With such small numbers of children it was difficult to reach comprehensive conclusions from any individual study. Although most studies of traumatic aphasias concluded that the prognosis for recovery was good in this group compared to the bad prognosis in studies of convulsive aphasias, it was difficult to see how these claims could be substantiated when few used the appropriate forms for longitudinal assessment of language problems and few actual language data were reported.

This led to the development of the following clinical picture of childhood ACA:

Traumatic aphasias	*Convulsive aphasias*
Short-term problem	Long-term problem
Complete recovery is the rule	Complete recovery is rare
Generally non-fluent aphasia	
A period of post-traumatic mutism	
Some comprehension problems	
Persistent word-finding problems	
Absence of paraphasias or jargon	
Some dyslexia and dysgraphia	Generally a severe receptive aphasia
	Described as a verbal auditory agnosia
	May be a gradual deterioration or acute onset with or without epilepsy

However, in 1978, the series reported by Woods and Teuber not only included one child with the unusual pattern of a fluent 'jargon' aphasia and severe comprehension problems, but proved to be a new starting point in the study of ACA. They tried to document the long-term recovery of the group using more suitable assessment techniques. This trend has continued, leading to reports of an increasing range of aphasic symptoms in ACA and including a wide range of paraphasias (Van Hout, Evrard and Lyon, 1985); it has also led to several other reports of fluent aphasias including those by Van Dongen, Loonen and Van Dongen (1985) and Van Dongen and Pacquier (1991).

Problems in the study of ACA

Although a brief overview, this chapter clearly shows some of the problems in the study of ACA. A more comprehensive review of previous studies relating to the specific aetiological groups is given in each chapter. In this chapter, some of the general problems in the study of ACA are discussed, together with some potential solutions.

Rarity of the problem

It has already been pointed out that ACA is a rare cause of language disturbance in childhood when compared with problems of developmental origin. However, most clinicians are also familiar with children who have a history of a short arrest or possible deterioration in early language development, which is sometimes associated with an illness or even a psychological event. There is clearly a grey area between clear cases of ACA preceded by a recognisable period of normal language development and those children who never develop normal language, in whom it is difficult to rule out some interference in language development. However, it is often difficult to establish specific evidence for this, and this group is considered in Chapter 7.

Here those clear-cut cases of ACA are dealt with, in which it has been possible to establish, even if usually by informal reports only, that the child had a period of normal, or near-normal, language development before the onset of the aphasia. The reported cases were all seen by the author and represent part of a larger group (over 80 cases) seen over 10 years. Such a group is by no means representative of an ordinary clinical caseload for the average speech and language therapist, but is the result of a research interest in this area. Bishop (1988) stated: 'Given the rarity of acquired aphasia in children, it is unlikely that progress will be made unless researchers start to co-operate in multi-centre studies'; this view has been well recognised by those working in this field in Europe. Although cooperative studies are still relatively new, this philosophy has led to the growth of a European study group and some joint work has been reported by Martins et al. (1991).

Inadequacy of language tests used

Bishop (1988) has also stated: 'In this field small numbers of subjects are inevitable, but poor measurement of language function is not'; however, time and time again studies have failed to report language function and aphasic symptoms in sufficient detail. Most early studies, such as that of Collignon, Hecaen and Angelergues (1968), relied on subjective reports of informal assessments and bedside observations of the aphasia. Where concern was expressed about long-term recovery of children with ACA, as in Alajouanine and Lhermitte (1965), reference to peer group norms was not given, and it was therefore impossible to determine what a good or poor recovery might have been. Bishop (1988) hoped that 'future studies will increasingly supplement clinical observation with objective and standardised measures'.

The cases reported in this book have been selected with this aim in view. However, the selection of appropriate assessment procedures can still be a problem for the inexperienced clinician seeing a child in a local clinic. We are all familiar with the clinical dilemma outlined by Coombes (1987): 'How to know what to do, what to do (including who to do it to and where), when to do it, when to stop.'

The first part of the process is the comprehensive assessment of the child to produce a detailed language profile. Lees and Urwin (1991) suggested that there were five major purposes for the comprehensive assessment of a child's language problem:

1. The establishment of a baseline of that child's language impairment.
2. From there to contribute to the setting up of an appropriate management plan.
3. To help the child, family and others come to terms with the history and implications of the condition.
4. To help in the recognition of the condition if it recurs, either in the same family or in others.
5. To allow longitudinal monitoring of the child's condition as well as between-child comparison in clinically based research.

However, it is not altogether obvious what assessment material would be most suitable for these tasks in children with ACA. Previous studies have often used tests that are designed for developmental problems (Huskisson, 1973), such as the Reynell Developmental Language Scales (RDLS) (Reynell, 1985), or tests designed for adults with aphasia. In many ways it is difficult to get away from some of these problems – there are so few tests that have been designed primarily for children with ACA.

Some tests are more suitable than others for use with ACA. The Test for Reception of Grammar (TROG: Bishop, 1983) was designed to assess children with language disorders including some with the Landau–Kleffner syndrome (Bishop, 1982), and is becoming quite widely used with this group. An informal study undertaken in 1986, among speech and language therapists in the UK who are seeing children with ACA, reported the TROG as the most widely used assessment tool. Some adult aphasia tests have been adapted for use with children by the addition of normal data for at least part of the age group. Gaddes and Crockett (1975) have produced norms for 6–13 year olds on the Spreen–Benton Aphasia Tests (Spreen and Benton, 1969), and Lees (1989) includes some norms for teenagers on the Graded Naming Test (McKenna and Warrington, 1983). The problem of appropriate assessment material will be discussed further as it arises in each chapter. The basic test procedure used for the cases reported throughout, and for the longitudinal study in Lees (1989), is outlined in Appendix I; the rationale underlying its adoption is also given there.

Lesion-based studies

The use of the lesion-based model has already been mentioned – from its basis in the work of Broca and Wernicke to its development by Goodglass and Kaplan (1972). Most of the early studies were based on this model, even when lesions could not be anatomically confirmed. With the development of neuroradiological techniques such as computed tomography (CT) scanning and magnetic resonance imaging (MRI), which have improved the identification of lesions, most studies have retained the use of this model, despite the fact that it does not provide a basis for understanding the pathology of those children not presenting with identifiable lesions. This includes most children with the Landau–Kleffner syndrome and other convulsive aphasias. It is also of limited application to children with closed head injury. Those with severe head injuries are likely to have bilateral lesions and those with more minor injuries may have areas of contusion and oedema that are a different type of cerebral injury, although they often lead to significant deficits.

A predominantly lesion-based perspective on ACA may also overlook the underlying, ongoing development of the child. With a model based on adult studies, it is all too easy to forget that both the child, and the child's brain, are still developing and maturing. This can lead to the child's needs and rights, particularly in educational terms, being overlooked.

A further criticism of the Goodglass and Kaplan (1972) model is that it is of limited application even in adults (Marshall, 1986). Although we clearly do need a model from which to develop and test our hypotheses, that model should not be so rigid as to rule out significant numbers of the children seen. If this is so then the model has clearly ceased to be applicable and must be discarded in favour of one that will help to generate new hypotheses. The Goodglass and Kaplan model can no longer be upheld as the major model for the study of aphasia, because it fails to explain significant numbers of aphasias in childhood. It must be replaced by a model that is not solely based on the position and extent of lesions. It is to be hoped that such a model may be developed through the clinical study of ACA.

The treatment effect and concept of recovery

Most early studies emphasised the good prognosis for recovery from ACA of traumatic origin, even though they could not measure the severity of the aphasia or provide peer group norms. In some studies this claim is clearly false. Alajouanine and Lhermitte (1965) reported that two-thirds of their 32 children had regained 'normal or nearly normal' language 1 year post-onset, and yet they went on to report severe residual motor problems, EEG abnormalities and problems at school with most of them. Such claims must lead to clinicians wondering what 'recovery' might be. Too many recent reports have concentrated on a return to a 'normal' score on one or more standardised tests, for example, Martins and Ferro (1991). However, it is often the lack of objective measures that has hindered our understanding. Complete recovery can only be claimed when a child is able to resume all activities, appropriate, both educationally and socially, to the peer group, and this requires a closer look at the child's learning abilities and quality of life. One of the problems with such a definition is that, from this a per-spective, it is probable that few children can really be said to make a complete recovery from ACA. The extent and severity of residual problems must be reported carefully and taken seriously if appropriate plans are to be made for the children's needs. Few studies have investigated any treatment effect in ACA, for reasons outlined here, and others relating to the whole range of problems that arise when setting up treatment studies in children. It is only when there is a clear picture of a child's residual deficits that clear aims and objectives for long- and short-term management can be produced. If treatment studies are to be set up then there must be a clearer understanding of recovery.

However, when considering the long-term recovery of a child, we cannot abstain from short-term intervention, even in the acute period. It is therefore important that the progress of children with ACA is documented as fully as possible at all stages of recovery. It is hoped that the cases presented here will demonstrate one way of doing that.

Management within a multidisciplinary team

As ACA usually arises from complex neurological conditions, most children will be seen by a range of professionals during their recovery. The child and family will be called upon to relate the history to many different individuals, each with a part to play in the child's management. For long-term well-being of the child and family, for ease of management and for development of a better understanding of ACA, a multidisciplinary team approach is to be recommended.

Professionals in different fields are often so concerned with the pressing needs of a child in their field of expertise that they find it difficult to take on board the point of view of other professionals. Consequently acute medicine professionals may fail to communicate with those on the therapy side, and both may fail to communicate with educational services. Such a state of affairs cannot be tolerated if the well-being of the child is of prime concern, and the aim should be to work as a multidisciplinary team with exchange of views and the development of a holistic picture of the child's needs – which is acted upon. This team will need a leader, but not the autocratic dictator of so many old hospital comedies. Also in order to work efficiently, a team needs to meet together regularly. A pattern and style of management need to be agreed and set up for each child, although there will be differences in the way this works, depending on the aetiologies and the recovery. The needs of the head-injured child in intensive care are obviously quite different from those of a child with Landau–Kleffner syndrome who is in special education – specific differences are referred to in the relevant chapters. Suffice it to emphasise that although the team members will vary according to the situation, the child and immediate family are always central members.

Assessment of speech and language in ACA

The clinician progresses towards 'knowing what to do' through the assessment procedure: each professional who sees the child with ACA will assess the situation from his or her perspective. Therefore, the speech and language data will just be part of the overall profile; this may be made up of information about neurological status, including investigations such as CT or MRI scan, and angiography or EEG, and assessments of mobility, hearing, neuropsychology etc. depending on the situation. The speech and language therapist needs to carry out a comprehensive assessment of the child's speech and language skills; these are evaluated and a profile drawn up of the child's strengths and weaknesses, on which future management may be based. This management protocol may not always be created by the speech and language therapist, for example, when an assessment has to be made on which a neurosurgeon may base surgical intervention or a paediatric neurologist may base anitconvulsant therapy. Choice of speech and language assessment procedures is determined by a number of factors: the child's age and level of ability; the presence of coexisting disabilities such as motor or perceptual problems; the assessment procedures available; the experience of the clinician; and the need for repetition of the assessment at any stage during recovery.

Cross and Ozanne (1990) outlined one possible model for the assessment of children with ACA, which included standardised tests, informal or non-standardised tests, and observations, as well as samples of spontaneous language and play. Within the area of language assessment, they use the form/content/use division of language to look at syntactic, semantic and pragmatic abilities and, additionally, reading, writing and speech production. They have given a comprehensive overview of a number of tests that could be used with this population. Another summary of a test procedure used with ACA can be found in Lees and Urwin (1991) who also reviewed a wide range of speech and language test material.

The actual tests a clinician may choose will depend on many things, but most often on the availability of different test procedures and her or his familiarity with these. A survey carried out in 1986 asked speech and language therapists seeing children with ACA in the UK about the assessment procedures they used. Collated results from 27 replies gave quite a long list of tests (Table 1.2).

What is interesting about this list is that it contains material designed for use with both children and adults, and that few of the tests were originally designed for this specific population. Of those listed, only two – the Test for Reception of Grammar (TROG) (Bishop, 1983) and the Children's Aphasia Screening Test (CAST) (Whurr and Evans, 1986) – could be said to fulfil these criteria. Bishop (1982) reported that her trial version of the TROG was used with a group of children with Landau–Kleffner syndrome whereas

Table 1.2 Assessments used by speech and language therapists seeing children with ACA in the UK*

Title	Author(s)
Test for Reception of Grammar (TROG)	Bishop (1983)
Frenchay Dysarthria Test	Enderby (1983)
Reynell Developmental Language Scales (RDLS) (revised)	Reynell (1985)
Children's Aphasia Screening Test	Whurr and Evans (1986)
English Picture Vocabulary Test	Brimer and Dunn (1973)
Symbolic Play Test	Lowe and Costello (1976)
Graded Naming Test	McKenna and Warrington (1983)
Porch Index of Communicative Ability in Children	Porch (1972)
Illinois Test of Psycholinguistic Abilities	Kirk, McCarthy and Kirk (1968)
Derbyshire Language Scheme	Knowles and Masidlover (1982)
Boston Aphasia Test	Goodglass and Kaplan (1972)
The Token Test for Children	Di Simone (1978)
Action Picture Test	Renfrew (1988)
Word Finding Vocabulary Test (WFVT)	Renfrew (1977a)
Receptive and Expressive Emergent Language Scale	Bzoch and League (1970)
Language Assessment, Remediation and Screening Procedure	Crystal, Fletcher and Garman (1989)

* Replies from 27 clinicians are given in order of preference, from a survey carried out by the author in 1986.

Whurr and Evans essentially adapted the adult version of Whurr's Aphasia Screening Test (Whurr, 1974) for use with children. They aimed to provide a simple yet sensitive test for identification of language disorder in brain-injured children. In the clinical situation it is more sensitive to the needs of younger children in the acute stages than for longer-term follow-up or for use with older children; in both these situations the test ceiling is often reached.

Of the adult tests used, the Frenchay Dysarthria Test (Enderby, 1983) was the most popular, which probably indicates the paucity of formal assessment techniques for investigation of oral dysfunction in children. It is to be hoped that the Paediatric Oral Skills Package (Brindley et al., 1993) will help to remedy this problem. This detailed observation schedule aims to look at all areas of oral function in children aged 0–16 years and can be used alongside other techniques such as radiological investigations to help create a detailed profile of a child's oral skills.

The assessment procedure used with the cases outlined in this book was developed in a clinical situation. Its aims were to provide as comprehensive an assessment of speech and language as possible within 30-45 minutes (considered to be the average time available for initial assessments), using tests that were suitable, wherever possible, for the age group under examination and familiar to most speech and language therapists (or at least not requiring a lengthy time to learn the test procedure); these tests also had peer group norms where possible, and could be repeated at regular intervals during the recovery process without compromising the validity of the tests.

Obviously, this does not cover all possibilities. New tests are continually becoming available. Some younger children or those with severe involvement of motor or perceptual skills may need to use adapted tests or even computerised assessment procedures. Similarly, where specific deficits are revealed, a more detailed procedure, which might be specific to the child, may have to be developed to assess the problem. For a general review of speech and language tests available, the reader is referred to summaries published elsewhere (Bishop and Mogford, 1988; Cross and Ozanne, 1990; Lees and Urwin, 1991).

The assessment of speech and language reported here formed the basis of the study of 34 children with ACA reported by Lees (1989). Longitudinal data from five children with ACA using the same battery of tests were reported by Lees and Neville (1990) and the tests are the following:

1. For auditory-verbal comprehension: the Test for Reception of Grammar (Bishop, 1983).
2. For confrontational naming: the Word Finding Vocabulary Test (Renfrew, 1977a) for children up to 10 years; the Graded Naming Test (McKenna and Warrington, 1983) for children over 11 years, using the norms of Lees (1989).
3. For naming by association: the Auditory Association subtest of the Illinois Test of Psycholinguistic Abilities (ITPA) (Kirk, McCarthy and Kirk, 1968).
4. For short-term auditory-verbal memory and repetition: the Sentence Repetition subtest (Spreen and Benton, 1969) using the norms of Gaddes and Crockett (1975).
5. A sample of expressive language was elicited using a story-telling technique (after Mandler and Johnson, 1977), the detailed description of which is in Appendix I (also in Lees and Neville, 1990; Lees and Urwin, 1991).

The results from these tests were evaluated both quantitatively and qualitatively. Tests scores were converted to z-scores and displayed graphically over time to show the child's progress during recovery. These test results are also used to determine the extent of the child's recovery. The z-scores on both the Test for Reception of Grammar and a naming test are used to predict outcome in comprehension and expressive language, respectively, according to the following classification:

Severity group	z-score
Normal-to-above average	Any score over 0
Normal-to-mild deficit	0 to -1
Moderate deficit	-1 to -2
Severe deficit	Any score below -2

This classification of severity was used to determine outcome in the longitudinal study (Lees, 1989) and has more recently been used in a study of outcome in children with developmental disorders by Haynes (1992).

Two tests that can include a qualitative analysis of errors are the Test for Word Finding (German, 1986) and the Test for Reception of Grammar (Bishop, 1983). Errors, such as delay in response time, number of self-correctional errors, number of repetitions a child requires, types and numbers of paraphasic errors, syntactic errors, perseverations, can all be coded and compared either during the child's progress or between children. However, to date, no normalised data are available in respect of qualitative errors for children with ACA. The need for clinicians to develop ways of recording qualitative assessment data in all types of childhood language disorder cannot be emphasised too much. When moving from assessment to treatment planning, it is often the quality of the child's responses and the types of cues a child uses that will be most helpful in promoting functional communication.

Some clinicians will find helpful the 16-point classification of responses used by Porch in the Porch Index of Communicative Ability in Children (PICAC; Porch, 1972). Others will be daunted by the size of this system. A 5-point method of recording qualitative assessment data was proposed by Lees and Urwin (1991) and was also used by Lees (1989):

1. All accurate and complete responses not requiring a repetition or cue will not receive any additional annotation (in other words, just score correct reponses according to the usual method on any specific test).
2. All complete and accurate reponses carried out after a delay of up to 10 seconds will be coded as B (this is an accurate but delayed response).
3. All complete and accurate responses carried out after the tester repeats the instructions will be coded as C.
4. All complete and accurate responses carried out after the child requests a repetition will be coded as C(i).
5. All responses that are complete and accurate after the child initially chooses another response and then changes her or his mind (a self-corrected response) will be coded as D.

Obviously this is not the only way of ordering such observations and clinicians are encouraged to develop a system that works for them, so that more data on the quality of children's responses during assessment, and also treatment, might be made available.

Classifying language disorders in childhood

A wide range of presenting language problems has been reported in ACA across aetiologies by various authors (Deonna et al., 1977; Van Hout, Evrard and Lyon, 1985). Severe receptive aphasia, the major feature of the Landau–Kleffner syndrome, can also be a feature of the acute phase of traumatic aphasia. Similarly word-finding problems and paraphasias can occur in both the traumatic and the convulsive groups.

A number of methods have been used to classify language deficits of language-impaired groups, and it would seem sensible to review the reasons for adopting a system that would allow for the classification of types of aphasia. The purpose of defining language disorder syndromes is: to outline natural history and substantiate prognosis; to allocate appropriate treatment and/or management; to enable appropriate comparisons between children; and to facilitate research.

The major classification used by those assessing aphasic adults was outlined by Goodglass and Kaplan (1972) (Table 1.3). Some authors have used this classification for children with acquired aphasias (Van Dongen, Loonen and Van Dongen, 1985; Martins and Ferro, 1987; Paquier et al., 1989). It is interesting to note here that studies of the use of this classification system in adult aphasia have found that between 30% and 50% of cases cannot be classified into one of these traditional syndromes (Marshall, 1986).

Reference to the Goodglass and Kaplan categories will demonstrate that, although they define aphasic symptoms according to a limited number of parameters, the overall descriptions are rather general and few specific indications of severity or level are given. The parameters used include a measure of verbal comprehension, naming (including vocabulary and the presence of paraphasias), sentence repetition and the fluency of expressive language. However, terms such as 'severe' are not defined objectively, i.e. in terms of a particular level or test score. Also no information is given about how the pattern of language deficit in these aphasic syndromes might change during recovery.

The problem of appropriate terminology for language disorders in childhood was addressed by Bishop and Rosenbloom (1987), who agreed that no consistent approach has yet been adopted. In developmental language disorder, six language disorder subtypes were proposed by Rapin and Allen (1987) (Table 1.4). Some of these language disorder subtypes have been compared to types of aphasic language disturbance seen in adults. In addition, they have been used to confirm that the communication disorders

Table 1.3 The main aphasic syndromes as described by Goodglass and Kaplan (1972)

Syndrome	Comment
Broca's aphasia	A non-fluent aphasia with awkward articulation, restricted vocabulary and grammar, and well-preserved auditory comprehension
Wernicke's aphasia	A fluent aphasia with impaired auditory comprehension, paraphasic speech and word-finding difficulty
Anomia	Severe word-finding problems; speech is fluent with few paraphasias
Global aphasia	Severe deficit in verbal comprehension, vocabulary and grammar with speech restricted to stereotyped utterances
Conduction aphasia	A fluent aphasia in which sentence repetition appears selectively impaired in relation to auditory comprehension
Transcortical sensory aphasia	A rare aphasia with severe deficit in verbal comprehension, normal or near normal sentence repetition, and severely impaired naming with paraphasias and perseverations and little extended expressive language
Pure word deafness or verbal auditory agnosia	No verbal comprehension
Mixed non-fluent aphasia	A tendency to non-fluent speech, moderate verbal comprehension problems but some expressive language

of children with developmental language disorders and autistic spectrum disorders are the same, but that the prevalence of the syndromes differs in the two groups.

Clearly, Rapin and Allen's categories also present some problems. Two of the categories are named with neurological aspects in mind: dyspraxia and agnosia. The other categories, however, contain strictly linguistic terms. As with Goodglass and Kaplan there is no attempt to give objective definitions of 'severe' or other similar terms, but they have attempted to describe the probable prognosis of each subtype with a brief description of the clinical picture that may be seen in an older child, although admittedly in very general terms. Although stating that the boundaries between the syndromes may be blurred, Rapin and Allen (1987) also said that this 'does not suggest to us that they are invalid or but variants of a single disorder with unequal

Table 1.4 Six language disorder subtypes as described by Rapin and Allen (1987)

Disorder subtype	Comment
Verbal auditory agnosia	Also called word deafness. There is no auditory-verbal comprehension. The problem is thought to have a poor prognosis and children need to be taught to understand language through the visual channel
Semantic-pragmatic deficit	Fluent and well-formed speech which initially is echolalic and delayed echolalia, progressing onto well learnt monologues. Auditory-verbal comprehension is literal and the child often responds to key words in the sentence. Other features of expressive language include verbal stereotypes, perseveration and circumlocution; said to have features of transcortical sensory aphasia
Lexical-syntactic deficit	A severe word retrieval difficulty alongside a difficulty forming connected utterances and understanding complex grammar. The child may produce paraphasias; said to share features with both anomia and conduction aphasia
Phonological-syntactic deficit	Speech is dysfluent in short utterances, usually with morphological errors. Comprehension may be impaired but less so than expression and phonological contrasts are reduced: said to be reminiscent of Broca's aphasia
Phonological programming deficit	Utterances are longer but there is a moderate-to-severe problem of speech intelligibility. Speech-sound contrasts are severely reduced
Verbal dyspraxia	Speech is very dysfluent and severely unintelligible. There is usually evidence of a motor planning deficit and possibly other more general motor deficits

severity, any more than the fuzzy edges of the acquired aphasias negate their validity'. I would suggest that the validity or otherwise of such syndromes is borne out both by the extent to which they provide a useful classification of language impairments and by the contribution they make to our understanding of these syndromes.

Although there has been an increase in the number of studies containing detailed clinical reports of the language profiles of ACA patients, there has been no consistent use of a classification system for these disorders, and the most commonly used system remains that developed by Goodglass and Kaplan (1972). There has only recently been any discussion (Lees, 1993) of how unsatisfactory this or any other classification system is for the subtypes of language disorder seen in ACA. In the Lees (1993) study the language profiles of 34 children with ACA, coming from a range of aetiologies, were compared with the categories of aphasia described by Goodglass and Kaplan (1972) and the language disorder subtypes of Rapin and Allen (1987), in order to see how many children had language deficits that could be classified according to these two systems.

Analysis of the profiles showed that 53% of the children could not be allocated to one of the Goodglass and Kaplan categories. Of those who could not be classified: four children presented with fluctuating aphasias which included periods of word deafness, anomia and Wernicke-type aphasia; eight had closed head injuries and, as a result, a slowing in speed of auditory verbal processing and lexical recall; and five others had short periods of paraphasias followed by mild word-finding problems. Similarly, 59% of the children could not be allocated to one of the Rapin and Allen subtypes; and of these the same four who had fluctuating aphasias had periods of verbal auditory agnosia and semantic–pragmatic deficit as well as severe word-finding problems. The remainder could be divided up as: thirteen head injured, showing a range of problems with the speed and volume of auditory verbal processing, auditory verbal comprehension problems, word-finding difficulties, including some paraphasias but no expressive phonological problems; two others with aphasic periods of short duration in which verbal comprehension problems and paraphasias were the most common features; and one with the Landau–Kleffner syndrome who appeared to pass through verbal auditory agnosia, semantic–pragmatic deficit and lexical–syntactic deficit. This study suggested that the classification of language deficits in acquired childhood aphasia cannot be adequately undertaken using either the Goodglass and Kaplan or the Rapin and Allen categories.

Marshall (1986), in his criticism of the use of the traditional classification of aphasic syndromes in adults, noted that 'all clinical definitions are replete with such words as "some", "typically", "often" and so forth' and further stated that perhaps we should accept that 'the classical taxonomy only accepts a minority of patients within its confines'. This may be so, and no doubt it will still be interesting to describe children with acquired aphasia whose symptoms concur with those syndromes seen in aphasic adults. However, the whole process by which we describe language disorder in children needs to be reconsidered. Rapin and Allen (1987) reported that their six language disorder subtypes accounted for types of language deficits seen in two groups of children with developmental language disorder and autism. The data presented by Lees (1993) suggested that the same subtypes were not so useful in classifying the language deficits of ACA. One factor that Rapin and Allen did not consider was the way in which the language disorder changed during the natural history; this is something that is perhaps more obvious in recovery from ACA. Also they do not accept the possible overlap between syndromes, where children seem to present with features of more than one subtype. Bishop and Rosenbloom (1987) concluded that 'we need more information about the time course, patterns of evolution and the natural and modified histories of children with language disorders' as they recognised that our present classificatory systems have largely been based on short-term observations and cross-sectional rather than longitudinal data.

Data from a longitudinal study of children with acquired aphasia (Lees and Neville, 1990) suggested that the language deficit may appear differently during the course of recovery. Even children with traumatic aphasia had an initial short period of word deafness, and those with fluctuating aphasias also had such repeated short periods. Recovery could include a period in which both literal comprehension prevails and jargon is produced. There was a gradual recovery of flexibility in auditory–verbal comprehension and a variable period in which paraphasias were produced. The final stage was often a high level problem involving speed and volume of auditory verbal processing and lexical recall. This description makes it clear that it is reasonable to expect these stages to need selective treatment or management. They described the use of a consistent assessment battery which allowed comparison across children of language recovery profiles. From a series of such profiles, it might be possible to hypothesise a classification that identifies the nature and course of the heterogeneous language deficits known as ACA better. The language profiles of all the cases in this book will be presented in this way, which will allow careful consideration to be given to this method. Although ACAs are related to aphasic syndromes in adults as well as to developmental language disorder, we would have better understanding of ACA if we respected this need for careful description rather than reliance on a classification set up for other conditions. This point will be addressed again in Chapter 8.

Understanding acquired childhood aphasia

In order to provide a comprehensive view of our present state of understanding of ACA, each of the chapters in this book will include the following:

1. The neuropathology of ACA as far as it is understood in relation to the different aetiologies.
2. The natural history of ACA as far as it has been recorded in respect of the different aetiologies. There are actually few longitudinal studies and this work will rely heavily on my own (Lees, 1989).
3. The management of ACA by speech and language therapists. This book aims to be of particular use to this group of professionals, although

hopefully not to the exclusion of others. In this respect it will build on the approach of Lees and Urwin (1991) in that it is 'concerned to demonstrate the value of a holistic clinical approach which includes the objective and logical alongside the subjective and intuitive', in the continued belief that this is how speech and language therapists actually work in clinical practice. However, it must also be recognised that it is not enough merely to state this view. We must also be prepared to discuss and criticise if we are to progress in our clinical work. Because there will be some similarities between subtypes in the assessment and management, some cross-referencing between chapters will be used to reduce repetition.

4. Other aspects of the management of ACA, particularly the team approach – most of the work reported is the result of working within a multidisciplinary team. It would therefore seem important to discuss ways in which such a team might work together for children with ACA, the role of some of the team members and any differences in management that might result from specific aetiologies.

5. Examples of children with ACA drawn from actual clinical practice. As wide a range as possible will be given of such examples within each aetiological group, including both typical and atypical cases. Where possible these will be presented longitudinally to show how ACA changes during recovery. The cases will be discussed in respect of the issues raised about each subtype.

6. Each chapter will end with a summary of the conclusions to be drawn about ACA in that particular group. These conclusions will be brought together in Chapter 8, which will address general issues related to the development of clinical practice and research arising from the material presented here.

Part I
Traumatic Aphasias

Chapter 2
Unilateral cerebral lesions of vascular origin

Pathology

Two kinds of pathology commonly occur: haemorrhage and infarction. Cerebral haemorrhage occurs when a cerebral blood vessel is ruptured and blood escapes into the brain. This may be into the subarachnoid space, into the substance of the brain or into the ventricles – called a subarachnoid, an intracerebral or an intraventricular haemorrhage respectively. Wherever the blood collects, a blood clot, or haematoma, may form. Obviously head trauma is a potential cause of bleeding within the brain. This will be considered in Chapter 3. In this chapter, types of cerebrovascular disease that lead to focal unilateral brain lesions are discussed.

Most speech and language therapists will be more familiar with the management of adult stroke survivors, which is more commonly the consequence of infarction. Infarction occurs when a cerebral vessel becomes blocked by a blood clot or thrombus, reducing or interrupting the supply of blood, and therefore oxygen in the blood, to the surrounding cerebral tissue.

Aphasia resulting from unilateral lesions of vascular origin is probably more common in adults than in children; the latter group should not, however, be ignored. For more than a century children with acute hemiplegia have been reported in the literature. Although this is a recognised sign of cerebral dysfunction, there has been much historical speculation about its causes in childhood. The advent of non-invasive vascular imaging rapidly clarified this subject; however, the presence of congenital hemiplegia, and sometimes other deficits, serves to complicate the issue further. When an infant presents with a mild hemiplegia, attributing this to prenatal or postnatal causes may take considerable investigation although most appear to be caused by intrauterine ischaemia or early embryological defects. The term 'cerebral palsy' is often used to refer to a wide range of motor disorders of varying severity in childhood. Cerebral palsy was defined by Bax (1964) as a disorder of movement and posture due to a defect or lesion of the immature brain. Both the lesion and the disorder are non-progressive and may arise in the prenatal period, at the time of birth or in the neonatal period. The subsequent discussion is not concerned with the motor and/or cognitive deficits of cerebral palsy, only the language deficit.

There has been considerable research into the long-term effects on speech and language development of early cerebral lesions, defined as those acquired before the age of 1 year. Bishop (1988) reviewed a great deal of this material, resulting from her interest in language development 'in exceptional circumstances'. She noted that 'we might expect to find that left-hemisphere damage early in life would preclude language development, but this is not so'. As early as 1897, Freud remarked on the rarity of persistent language disturbances in children with congenital right hemiplegia. In more recent research an experimental design has often been used which has compared groups of children with early (acquired before 1 year of age) focal lesions of either the left or right hemispheres with groups of children with late (acquired after 1 year of age) focal lesions of either hemisphere. The children are then asked to carry out different types of tasks, whether linguistic, visuospatial or other cognitive tasks, and results are used to decide whether or not there is evidence of specific effects of early and late brain lesions and also whether or not there is evidence to support the hypothesis that the left cerebral hemisphere has a predisposition for dominance in language development before and after birth. Such studies have been carried out by many authors including Vargha-Khadem, O'Gorman and Watters (1985), Aram and Ekelman (1988a,b), Aram and Aram (1991b) and Riva et al. (1991). Most have supported the hypothesis that the left hemisphere is so predisposed in the development of language.

Of the more recent studies some have looked at quite specific aspects of functioning. Eisele (1991) carried out a detailed study of language comprehension, using two groups of children with unilateral lesions to right and left hemispheres respectively and two control groups individually matched for age, sex and race to the children in the first groups. The onset of the cerebral lesions ranged from the perinatal period to 9 years of age, but none of the children was clinically aphasic at the time of the study. The children were asked to make 'truth-value judgements' on ten complex sentence types which were chosen to 'involve the integration of syntax as well as semantic and pragmatic language knowledge', with the aim of demonstrating whether or not subtle aspects of language function might be impaired by early right hemisphere injury as well as demonstrating the more usually reported effects on language of early left hemisphere injury. Eisele claimed that her results did uphold this hypothesis and went on to conclude, not surprisingly perhaps, that 'a complete acquisition of language depends on the normal functioning of both hemispheres throughout the course of development'.

However, it is my intention to discuss in more detail those children who present with acute aphasia in childhood, with or without hemiplegia, resulting from cerebrovasular disease – both vascular malformations and cerebrovascular occlusion disorders. The various subtypes of these conditions have been well documented by Isler (1971) who presented a wide range of cases and considered both the neurological management and the prognosis of each.

Few other studies have considered this aetiological group exclusively, and none from the specific point of view of presenting speech and language disorder, apart from a single case of Dennis (1980). In most studies of such ACA children, the unilateral cerebrovascular disease is mixed with other traumatic aetiologies so glossing over the underlying neuropathological mechanisms and their different effects. It is acknowledged that these disorders are a rare cause of morbidity and mortality in the first two decades of life (Kelly, Mellinger and Sundt, 1978). Isler (1971) and Kelly, Mellinger and Sundt (1978) both agree that the sex ratio of incidence indicates that boys are almost twice as likely as girls to present with arteriovenous malformations, although in *Moyamoya* syndrome – a disorder associated with multiple intracranial arterial occlusions and caused by a range of pathologies – Isler's review of the literature demonstrated that it was more common in girls.

Natural history

The effect of an acquired vascular lesion on a child's language does appear to vary considerably from one child to another. Factors, such as the site of the lesion, the age at which the lesion is acquired and the initial severity of the disorder, have been suggested as the major variables related to prognosis. The way in which these variables interact is not understood but, as with developmental language disorder, it is obviously far from simple. In defining ACA, it is usual to include only those children whose cerebral lesions were obviously acquired after spoken language had become established. As already stated, children with congenital lesions may be included in the group described as having cerebral palsy, but they may also occasionally be included with children having developmental language disorders. Recent research has considered the long-term effects of early unilateral cerebral lesions, but few cases of severe language disorder in childhood have been reported. Case 1 is an example of a boy with a unilateral cerebral lesion arising in the neonatal period who presented with a developmental language disorder. The definition of ACA does of course leave a grey area, occurring roughly between 6 and 18 months of age, when it is difficult to decide whether a child should be considered as having an acquired problem or not. Some cases of anomalous aphasias, in which periods of regression and deterioration of communication skills in early childhood have been observed, will be considered in Chapter 7.

Except in some individual cases, few studies have specifically documented the natural history of aphasia subsequent to unilateral cerebral lesions. As these are highly variable only preliminary conclusions can be drawn. First, acute expressive aphasia appears to be rare in childhood. In most reported cases, where the results of formal language tests are included, the presence of comprehension disorders, as well as expressive language difficulties, has been clearly demonstrated. Second, a general picture of an initial period of relatively fast recovery, gradually tailing off, has also been shown (Lees and Neville, 1990); the extent of this period is a major determinant in final outcome. Lees (1989) suggested that prognosis is usually good in cases where children tested for verbal comprehension up to 6 months post-onset reached the level of -2 standard deviations from the mean. Those failing to reach this level were more likely to have significant long-term language deficits.

Paraphasic naming errors have been reported in children with unilateral cerebral lesions. Three types of paraphasia are usually recognised: semantic paraphasias where the error is semantically related to the target item (a 'table' is named as a 'chair'); phonemic paraphasias where the error is phonemically related to the target item (a 'thimble' is called a 'thrimble'); and neologisms where so many phonemic errors occur that it impossible to see any relationship between the error and the target item.

Van Hout, Evrard and Lyon (1985) documented a series of patients, not all of whom had the same aetiology, with a wide range of paraphasias, which had both temporary initial features of the aphasia and more persistent long-term problems. In the 11 children aged between 4 and 10 years, semantic or phonemic paraphasias always occurred. The tendency to perseverate these naming errors was also reported as a frequent occurrence. They postulated that the lack of previous reports of paraphasia in such cases of ACA (essentially the view before 1978) may have been the result of the fact that language investigations were not always carried within a reasonable period. Where the paraphasic period was short (perhaps only a few days) they would therefore have been missed. Clinical experience of following children from acute onset to long-term follow-up supports the view that detailed assessment at all stages of recovery is important for a full understanding of ACA. Lees (1989) reported that most children in that study who were in this aetiological group produced paraphasic errors at some time during the recovery period. These data further supported the work of Van Hout, Evrard and Lyon (1985), who found that a paraphasic period of more than 6 months was a poor prognostic sign.

Role of the speech and language therapist

A comprehensive assessment procedure will be required to determine the child's strengths and needs. Various tests and informal measures have been advocated. Dennis (1980) used the Neurosensory Centre Comprehensive Examination for Aphasia (Spreen and Benton, 1969) with the norms for children prepared by Gaddes and Crockett (1975). It may be useful to select some of these sub-tests to investigate specific functions such as naming, repetition, fluency or reading. It is only necessary to use the whole test battery in specific situations. Dennis (1980) also advocated the use of the story-telling techniques proposed by Mandler and Johnson (1977) for the analysis of expressive language. This can be useful when the child is reticent, particularly after a period of mutism which can be observed following stroke. These techniques have been used in other studies (Lees and Neville, 1990). Unfortunately peer group norms are not available.

A review of studies of children presenting with traumatic aphasias reveals the use of a wide range of assessment material. Aram (1991a) reviewed this subject, suggesting a number of different tests, but the list had a predictably North American bias. Several studies have used tests originally designed for the assessment of adult aphasia; for some tests peer group norms for children are available, e.g. the Spreen–Benton test, or there is a child's version, e.g. the Token Test (Di Simoni, 1978). However, many use the Boston Diagnostic Aphasia Examination (Goodglass and Kaplan, 1972) together with their own diagnostic categories. A discussion of the limitations in using such a system is provided in Chapter 1.

There are three levels at which the language of aphasic children can be evaluated: clinical rating, psychometric assessment and linguistic study. Each level requires a different amount of time for completion; each also provides different types and quantities of data; equally each may require a different amount of training in use. However, as Aram (1991a) concluded, 'whatever level of description used or specific tests selected or developed, the overwhelming conclusion that emerges . . . is that as an area of study, we have only begun to describe and understand factors related to the language of brain lesioned children'. It is impossible to know which tests suit which subgroups of aphasic children, until speech and language therapists give more detailed reports of their language in relation to different aetiological groups.

In the determination of the need for intervention directed at the child's naming difficulties, it is important to analyse the types of cues the child uses, whether they are self-generated or supplied by others. Children and adults with no language problems use self-generated and environmental cues to aid naming when necessary. It is possible to help aphasic children regain understanding of cueing; this, in turn, could improve naming. Appendix I gives some details of the cues used by normal teenagers doing the Graded Naming Test (McKenna and Warington, 1983). Through observation of which cues the child finds most helpful, a programme can be prepared which reinforces these over a range of individual and group tasks for confrontational and association naming, as well as in spontaneous language. Initially, tasks will involve naming in a structured but non-pressurised situation. Gradually the structure can be altered to include recall of names in other situations, ranging from more informal tasks to formal timed tasks. Children should, if feasible, be encouraged to keep a notebook to record situations in which naming has proved difficult; this can be used for later discussion with the therapist, and, using role-play, be re-enacted so that the children can work through the range of strategies that would help naming in a similar situation.

Other aspects of management

For those children admitted with acute aphasia arising from unilateral cerebral lesions, various investigations may be used to determine the aetiology, although the investigations used by the acute medical team will depend on the local situation. More readily available investigations include computed tomography (CT) and angiography. Magnetic resonance imaging is being used increasingly in children for better definition of damaged brain; non-invasive vessel imaging is also being used more. Occasionally investigations of cerebral vascular disorders can cause stroke-like syndromes, so angiography may not be indicated in all cases. However, when used the angiogram can provide a radiological picture of the cerebral vessels, so showing up any malformations present. Figure 2.1 is an example of an angiogram of a child with a large congenital arteriovenous malformation on the surface of the left cerebral hemisphere (see Case 21 for further details). CT scans of the brain provide a different type of radiograph which gives information about the density of the cerebral matter. They are able to demonstrate haemorrhage, infarction, haematoma or neoplasm, and will show, for example, whether there has been either general atrophy of the cerebral hemispheres or a shift in the position of the lateral ventricles. Figure 2.2 is a CT scan of a child with a large haematoma in the posterior part of the left temporal lobe caused by a haemorrhage of a congenital arteriovenous malformation (see Case 3 for further details).

There are two other imaging techniques that are slowly becoming available for the investigation of children with cerebral dysfunction: magnetic resonance imaging (MRI) and positron emission tomography (PET). As with CT, MRI is a non-invasive investigative technique. However, MRI is said to have several advantages over CT for investigations in children, including a greater sensitivity to blood flow, oedema, haemorrhage and the extent of

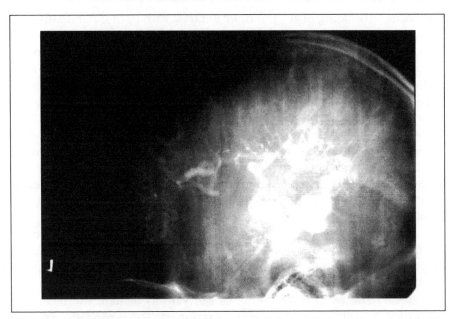

Figure 2.1 Angiogram of Case 21

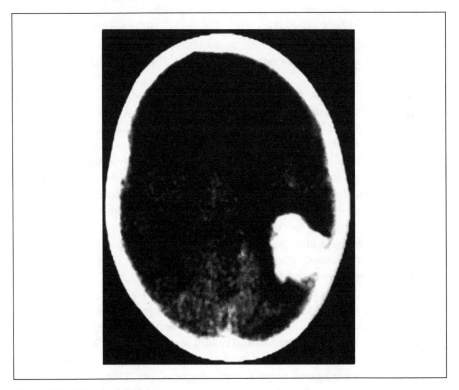

Figure 2.2 CT scan of Case 3

myelination (Gooding et al., 1984). By contrast with both CT and MRI, PET allows the study of brain physiology and chemistry: cerebral blood flow and oxygen or glucose metabolism can be examined. Metter (1987) reported the use of PET to investigate cerebral physiology in 70 adult aphasic patients and identified five abnormal patterns of activity. He claimed that the results showed that not only cortical but also subcortical connections were vital for competent language function. This technique has not been used extensively in ACA and as yet no comparable study exists in children. However, Robinson (1992) reviewed studies of using PET in aphasia and concluded that it is 'for very good reason why everyone is rethinking the neuro-physiology of language, not in terms of the strict one-to-one site-to-function relationship' of the lesion-based model but 'in terms of functionally over-lapping networks'.

A number of other deficits may occur with unilateral cerebrovascular lesions, particularly motor or sensory deficits. Where the lesion is in the posterior part of the temporal lobe, visual field defects may occur, whereas a more anterior lesion encroaching on the motor cortex can lead to hemiplegia. The severity of the latter can vary to include the face, arm and/or leg. Equally variable recovery is reported. The three girls reported later in this chapter (Cases 3, 4 and 5) provide good examples of the variablity of the presenting deficits and their duration. Thorough assessment by a number of different professionals is necessary to establish the extent of any coexisting problems, including audiological and ophthalmological investigations, as well as assessment by a physiotherapist and occupational therapist.

In the long term, the child is likely to need assessment for educational placement. It is not sufficient to presume that children who can walk can return to their previous schools with no further discussion. Even if children make good recovery (i.e. scores return to within -2 standard deviations within 6 months of onset), it is advisable to have an annual follow-up for at least 2 years post-onset to rule out any specific educational needs. Very little is known about the long-term learning capacities of children who sustain unilateral cerebrovascular lesions, and certainly not enough to presume that any fast initial recovery curve will indicate a return to previous learning abilities. Therefore some level of surveillance up to school leaving age is a sensible precaution, and would begin to provide some of the information that is lacking for these children.

From clinical experience with children placed in a wide range of edu-cational situations, it has been found that the greatest benefit for a child with special educational needs that have been identified is close co-operation between the education and health services and with the family. In fact, some education authorities make creative attempts to meet these children's needs with good results (for example, Case 3). In other situations special educational needs are not properly identified and the child has an ongoing experience of failure and frustration (for example, Case 5). General rules cannot be made about specific educational provision for these children. Rather, comprehensive assessment of each individual is required so that each one has a profile of strengths and needs that can be translated into aims, goals and strategies – this has to be the right of every child.

Examples of children with unilateral cerebral lesions

Case 1

This case is a boy with a developmental language disorder from neonatal stroke. This boy (first described by Lees and Urwin, 1991) was born at 34 weeks' gestation, the second child of two healthy unrelated parents. At 29 weeks of pregnancy there was a history of a small amount of bleeding which did not, however, give cause for further concern. His birth weight was 2.3 kg which meant that he was rather small for dates. His parents began to be concerned when his motor development appeared different from his older, healthy and normally developing brother. At the age of 6 months a right hemiplegia was confirmed. He also had eczema but was otherwise well. A CT scan showed atrophy of the left cerebral hemisphere. There was an area of low density in the posterior part of the left frontal lobe in the region of Broca's area, and other smaller patches in the left temporal and parietal lobes which suggested an old left middle cerebral artery infarct. With physiotherapy his motor skills improved. He walked independently at 26 months.

Parental concern increased when it was noted that he was not speaking at 26 months, although his comprehension appeared good. Formal testing, using the Reynell Developmental Language Scales (revised) (Reynell, 1985) confirmed that comprehension was within normal limits for the age 2;6 years and remained so throughout the period he received speech and language therapy. He was using a few vowel sounds to communicate as well as pointing and pulling. A programme of therapy, which included the Makaton Vocabulary (Walker, 1980), was introduced and he soon learnt a useful number of signs. Despite his hemiplegia he managed to sign quite well and within 2 months was making up his own signs and linking signs accompanied by vowel sounds. He was over 3 years old before he developed a small vocabulary of single words, which were simple combinations of long vowels and glottal stops that had to be clarified by signing. Over the next year he received speech and language therapy twice weekly on an individual basis and once weekly in a small group. He made good progress with communication and became more verbal as he mastered first velar and then bilabial, nasal and plosive sounds. Signing remained vital for intelligibility.

He was admitted to a preschool language unit at the age of 4 years. By this stage his verbal language consisted of a wide vocabulary of open syllables in which the consonant-vowel combinations were predominantly plosives or nasals with long vowels and some glides. These were joined in short sequences of three of four words, often with glottal stops between each one. He continued to rely on signing to augment his communication. Figure 2.3 shows the profile of his recovery.

For this child, it is clear that the normal sequence of speech-sound acquisition was disrupted, resulting in a severe difficulty in communication through verbal language. Although it is not possible to relate all of this deficit to the early cerebral injury, it is difficult to suggest that it played no part in the aetiology of the problem. The case confirms that early lesions of

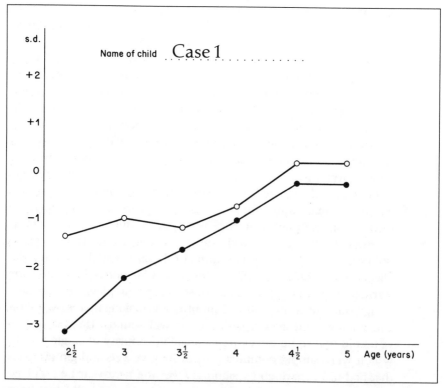

Figure 2.3   Profile of recovery of Case 1: (○) receptive language; (●) expressive language

the left cerebral hemisphere and Broca's area can interfere with language acquisition to the extent of affecting a child's educational needs. Careful study of children presenting with early unilateral cerebral lesions that involve areas thought to be primary for language processing is recommended.

Generally it has been considered that children having unilateral cerebral lesions with an onset before the age of 5 years recover quickly and well provided there are no other complications. It is probably more helpful to say that each child requires consistent long-term follow-up well into school age to determine the rate and extent of recovery, as demonstrated by the following example.

Case 2

This boy presented with an acute aphasia at the age of 4;5 years. He had a history of normal development, although his parents had recently become concerned about the persistence of a developmental dysfluency; they had seen a speech and language therapist about this. For 2 days before his admission, his parents had noticed that his face was slightly asymmetrical with his mouth turned down on the right side. His behaviour was also described as 'odd': he would walk around aimlessly, and appeared quiet and uninterested in play. On admission he was found to have a moderate right hemiplegia and an acute aphasia – his speech was slurred and expressive language was reduced to jargon. A CT scan confirmed a small lesion in the region of the left middle cerebral artery in the anterior part of the left temporal lobe.

His right hemiplegia gradually resolved over 4 days. There was no evidence of visual field defects and hearing was normal. During the first week the jargon persisted and he communicated by pointing, pulling and other gestures. He was producing neologisms and paraphasias as well as perseverated errors. Formal testing using the Test for Reception of Grammar (Bishop, 1983) confirmed a severe comprehension deficit.

However, by the second week his language showed a marked improvement and he was no longer using jargon. Comprehension was still impaired, as was naming. There was evidence of sentence formulation problems in expressive language. By 6 months post-onset, scores for both verbal comprehension and naming had regained the norm. However, there was still some evidence of grammatical problems in expressive language and some naming difficulties. Examples of his expressive language shown in Table 2.1 indicate the improvement over the 2 years of follow-up. Initially, there was evidence of unintelligible jargon and incomplete sentences which developed into a more non-fluent pattern; later this resolved with some minor grammatical errors. He began his education in a mainstream nursery class without additional support at the expected time. Only long-term follow-up will confirm whether this period of language disturbance will have a significant effect on his communication and, more especially, on his ability to acquire written language skills.

The expressive language samples in Table 2.1 show the gradual expansion of his telegrammatic utterances over 2 years, as well as a resolution of unintelligibility. Residual features of non-fluency at 2 years post-onset were predominantly excessive pausing and repetition of phrase structure. The graph of his overall language recovery is shown in Figure 2.4.

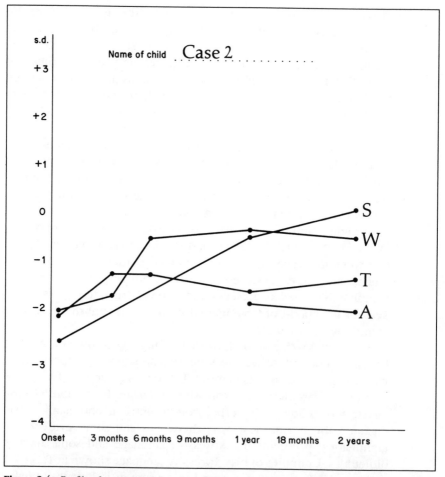

Figure 2.4 Profile of recovery of Case 2: A, auditory association; S, sentence repetition; T, TROG; W, Word Finding Vocabulary Test

Table 2.1   Examples of responses for Case 2 on the Action Picture Test*

Onset (age 4;5 years)
1. That's her ... doing ... cuddling teddy
2. Putting her /dɒz/ on
3. He got stuck /tʌt/
4. The man ... doing a lot of jumps
5. Did the ... er ... cat did
6. Her ... [unintelligible]
7. I don't know
8. The man ... doing lots of jobs
9. Happen to his shoe
10. They ... [unintelligible]

Three months post-onset (4;9 years)
1. There's a girl and a panda bear
2. There's a girl ... she's putting his sandals on ... it's snowy time
3. It goes next to there ... he pushed him
4. Jumping the horse ... he's a policeman
5. He feed the cats ... he feed the mouse
6. He got broken glasses ... he fellen down the stairs
7. Putting the letter ... post ... it's a boy
8. Laddering the cats
9. He got his slippers off
10. He got fall the apples ... the girl fall the apple ... that's the road

Six months post-onset (4;11 years)
1. Girl got her teddy bear
2. Putting his boots on 'cos it's snowing
3. Going to get that wall off him ... someone take him
4. Man going to jump the horse and the gate
5. Cat going to get mice
6. He fell over and broke his glasses
7. Going to lift him up 'cos he's going to put post up
8. The man is going ... climb up ladder ... and get the cat
9. Boy's crying ... lost his slipper ... the dog take it
10. Apples ... the boy put apples ... the lady carry the bag ... she dropping apples
    ... the boy doing picking apples

One year post-onset (5;8 years)
1. Cuddling ... she put her hands round her and cuddle the baby
2. Putting her boots in ... she's pulling her chair and she's rocking it backwards
   and she's fell off the chair
3. He get ... he some ... naughty boys tie him round 'cos he don't want to bite
   every children
4. He's jumping over the fence
5. He's chasing the mouse over the track
6. Fallen down step and broken his glasses
7. She's put the post in

Table 2.1 Continued

8. The man's doing ... he's got a ladder and he's fixing the roof and trying to get the cat away from it
9. He's taking his slipper and he's crying
10. She's dropped some apples and he pick the apples up

Two years post-onset (6;7 years)
1. She's cuddling a teddy 'cos she likes it
2. She's putting her boots on 'cos she's going outside ... or to the farm
3. He's tied round 'cos the man doesn't want the dog to go away. He's car parked there while he gets some dog food
4. He's having a race jumping over the gate
5. He's chasing the mouse 'cos he wants to eat them with his claws
6. She fell over by accident ... She's broken 'cos she fell over ... 'cos she broke her glasses
7. Putting the letter ... posting 'cos he can't reach it ... 'cos it's high for him that's why she lift him up
8. He's climbing up so he can get the cat down from his roof
9. He's crying 'cos that dog got his slipper
10. The lady brought a apple and it's dropping out of her ... and that boy picked it up and he told the lady there's a hole in ... and he picked them up to give them to the lady who dropped them

* Renfrew (1988).

In order to demonstrate the variability within this group, three girls who had lesions of the left hemisphere at different ages, all of which resulted in a severe acute aphasia, are presented next (Cases 3, 4 and 5). They all recovered differently, further confirming the way in which the complex interaction of varibles such as age at onset, lesion size and site occurs in children with ACA. The first, and the eldest, girl did very well to recover from a complete aphasia at the age of 13 years. At the age of 17 years she had a mild high-level language problem in the speed and volume of process- ing and recall, and a risk of epilepsy. The second girl recovered well in terms of language skills but had a residual right hemiplegia. However, the later stages of assessment showed that she was unable to learn at the same rate as her peers and so she did not return to mainstream school. The third girl, although similar in age to the second, showed the least recovery of language and also had a severe right hemiplegia. Their recovery profiles (Figures 2.5–2.7) are placed together so the patterns can be compared more easily. They are not intended to represent all the possible outcomes for this group, but to highlight the inadequacy of considering any one variable, in this case age, for determination of the eventual outcome.

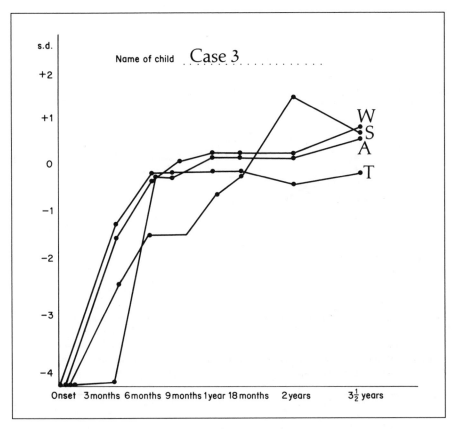

Figure 2.5   Profile of recovery of Case 3: A, auditory association; S, sentence repetition; T, TROG; W, Word Finding Vocabulary Test

Case 3

This girl (first described by Lees and Neville, 1990) had a normal developmental history when she presented with an acute aphasia at 13 years of age. CT scan and angiography revealed a large posterior temporoparietal haemorrhage from an arteriovenous malformation (see Figure 2.2). There was a right hemianopia and mild incoordination on the right.

Initially, she had a severe deficit in both receptive and expressive language – comprehending only single nouns and producing both semantic and phonemic paraphasias. Pure-tone audiometry confirmed normal hearing. On discharge from hospital she continued to receive speech and language therapy once weekly from her local service for a year. Eleven months post-onset she was readmitted with a small episode of language disturbance following a severe and prolonged headache, and some right-sided signs. There was a deter-

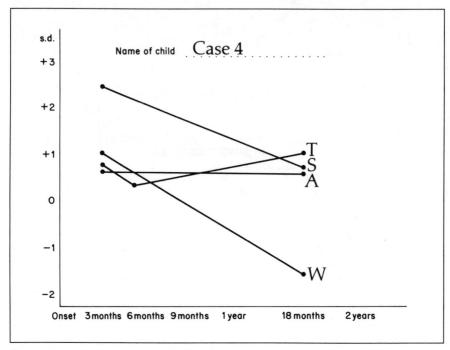

Figure 2.6 Profile of recovery of Case 4: A, auditory association; S, sentence repetition; T, TROG; W, Word Finding Vocabulary Test

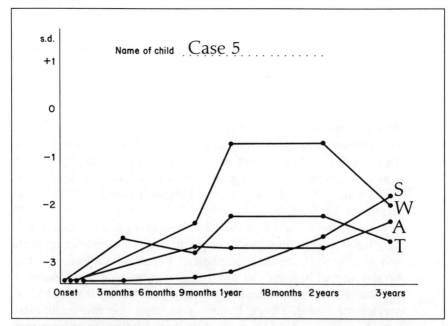

Figure 2.7 Profile of recovery of Case 5: A, auditory association; S, sentence repetition; T, TROG; W, Word Finding Vocabulary Test

ioration in her auditory–verbal processing and an increase in para-phasias. This resolved within 1 week. Two years after the initial event, another short episode of the same kind occurred. She was treated with carbamazepine and had stereotactic radiotherapy to a residual piece of the original arteriovenous malformation deep in the left temporal lobe. Her full-scale WISC IQ (Wechsler, 1974) 1 month after the first episode was 76, and 1 year later it had improved to 96.

She had a statement of educational needs which made provision for a personal tutor and integration to mainstream comprehensive school. By the age of 17 years she had passed three GCSE examin-ations and was studying for three more. She continued to experi-ence high level difficulties in the verbal comprehension of complex instructions in a noisy environment and occasional word-finding problems. She continued to take anticonvulsants.

During the course of her aphasia she did produce a range of paraphasias, which were predominantly phonemic; an increase in these always accompanied subsequent episodes. Some examples of these phonemic paraphasias include: (2 months post-onset) 'scare-crow' was called 'scarescrow', 'handcuffs' were 'handcrups', 'sporran' was called 'skoran'. Similar errors occurred over the next 2 years but never more than this number in one session.

Expressive language in a story-telling task was always non-fluent as this example of the Dog Story at 3 months post-onset shows:

'There was a dog and he wented down to the canal and he walked a p...
[six attempts at this] plank. And he went down.. he and with his piece of
... meat and he looked into the .... canal and he saw his new...he saw
his own reflection. He thought it was another dog and he ... did sort of
throw... he dived in dived in and he never s... and he never saw his meat
again.'

Case 4

This girl, with a normal developmental history, presented at age 8;2 years with an acute aphasia. She had had an influenza-like illness and headache for 3 days. Examination revealed a dense right hemiplegia and complete aphasia. This was diagnosed as a left middle cerebral artery infarct after a ruptured angioma of the left internal carotid artery, and was confirmed with CT scan and angiography. She was aphasic for 1 month during which time she was unable to com-prehend anything that was more than a single word. She then had a 6-month period producing paraphasic errors during which time the hemiplegia persisted. She also dribbled out of the right corner of her mouth. Up to 1 year after the event she continued to have word-finding and spelling difficulties. Pure-tone audiometry confirmed normal hearing. Her IQ on the WISC was 83 (Performance 94 and Verbal 74). Eighteen months post-onset her aphasia appeared to have resolved to a high level word-finding deficit, with comprehension being essentially normal. The right hemiplegia persisted. She was placed in a school for children with physical difficulties.

Her response to a story-telling task confirms that expressive language regained a good level of fluency and accuracy within 6 months of onset as shown in this example of the Dog Story:

> 'There was a dog and he had a piece of meat and he was going home. As he was going home he had to cross a bridge. When he looked down he could see his own reflection but he didn't know it was his reflection. So he opened his mouth to snap at the other piece of meat. His piece of meat was gone.'

Although conversation was a little more stilted it was not grossly impaired, as shown in this short speech about her holiday recorded 6 months post-onset:

> 'There are small countries. There are some countries that are smaller ... hotter than England; Jamaica, Barbados, St Kitts. Do you know any more? [hesitation here] America is hotter but it's too hot to stay outside and sunbathe. And I've been to Disney World.'

Case 5

This girl (first described by Lees and Neville, 1990) had a normal developmental history when she presented with an acute aphasia and a right hemiplegia at the age of 8;3 years. CT scan and angiography revealed severe arterial disease involving the left terminal internal carotid, left proximal middle cerebral artery and distal middle cerebral artery, with a large infarct. Pure-tone audiometry confirmed a conductive hearing loss of long standing of less than 30 dB. She had severe receptive and expressive aphasia so that she did not even respond to single words; and she was essentially anomic. There was some improvement in all areas, but 3 years post-onset she remained severely language disabled. She continued to receive speech and language therapy on a weekly basis from her local service for 2 years post-onset. Six months post-onset, her WISC IQ was recorded as Performance 86 and Verbal 52. No alternative provision for her educational needs was made by the local authority and she continued in a mainstream comprehensive school where she made poor progress. Her right hemiplegia persisted unchanged.

She produced very little language, and was particularly reluctant to name items to confrontation. Therefore few naming errors were recorded and the few given here suggest a general naming impairment: (at 3 months post-onset) 'basket' was called 'purse' as was 'case'; 'saw' was called 'knife'.

Very little spontaneous expressive language ever occurred but some short phrases were produced in a story-telling situation. This example of the Farmer Story was recorded 9 months post-onset:

> 'The farmer and the donkey go in barn. He pushed him..... He pulled him........ no go. Tell the cat scratch dog. Cat scratch him. Dog bark. He went in barn.'

Conclusions

Clearly simple conclusions cannot be drawn about age of onset and duration or severity of aphasia. The traditional view that unilateral cerebrovascular lesions in childhood rarely have significant long-term effects is not upheld by recent studies. However, the range and extent of recovery seen are highly variable and the way in which the numerous variables interact to influence recovery is not understood. Although there are a few studies that suggest that the interaction of the variables of age, extent and nature of lesion, type and severity of initial aphasia determines prognosis in this group (Loonen and Van Dongen, 1990; Martins and Ferro, 1991; Van Hout, 1991), in many respects it would be helpful to pool data across a number of centres to improve our understanding. Few centres have sufficient children to provide useful studies of this group. However, to be able to pool data, there must be agreement about a protocol; such a protocol is proposed in Appendix II. Unlike the adult group, there have been very few studies of treatment in children. Lees (1989) noted that the children in that study received varying amounts of speech and language therapy and it was therefore not possible to draw any conclusions about such therapy. It is likely that without multicentre studies, comprehensive long-term assessment and detailed case studies, any conclusions about the efficacy of therapy will remain unresolved.

Chapter 3
Head injury

Pathology

The largest group of children with acquired language problems are those who suffer head injuries of various severities. Middleton (1989) reported that the number of children with head injuries has been rising annually. Although severe injuries are known potentially to produce profound long-term effects, the view that mild injuries, which do in fact predominate, do not produce significant cognitive or psychological sequelae is now being challenged. As Middleton (1989) said 'children, once seen as having an advantage over adults with regard to recovery, may in fact be more vulnerable and have a poorer prognosis'. Despite this, adequate rehabilitation facilities are still not available in the UK for children who survive head injuries.

Most of the early mixed series of ACA (1942–1978) included a substantial number of head-injured children. In most of these series there was little attempt to differentiate between the possible underlying neuropathology and its implication for prognosis. More recent studies have recognised some of these implications and have given more details of the aetiological sub-groups in mixed studies (Loonen and Van Dongen, 1990).

According to Ewing-Cobbs et al. (1985), head injury is the most common cause of death in children. Middleton (1989) reported that four children in every 10 000 die from head injury in the UK every year. Ewing-Cobbs et al. (1985) discussed the mechanisms of trauma and the response of the injured brain. Although diffuse cerebral injury at impact is the major initial effect, other forces of acceleration, shearing and stretching occur subsequently, resulting in widespread injury to the cerebral tissues. This damage is sometimes shown up by advanced radiological techniques such as MRI.

Few studies have documented the recovery of cognitive and language skills in head-injured children. A series of 100 children under 19 years of age with severe head injuries was reported by Ward and Alberico (1987), and is an example of such studies. Severe head injury was defined by a score on the Glasgow Coma Scale of less than 7 on admission. Ninety-four per cent of the children had intracranial pressure monitoring and 24% of them died from their injuries, whereas 68% were said to have had a good or only moderately disabled outcome. However, the parameters were not defined further. The resolution of acute neurology is only a small measure of recovery in children who have sustained complex brain injury. Long-term neuropsychological deficits are more likely to affect the quality of life, the return to the former community and progress within the school; therefore these must be more carefully defined.

Since the early 1980s the number of children with acquired language problems after head injury referred has increased. This seems to be due to two factors: first better intensive care facilities, including the use of intra-cranial pressure monitoring, leading to more child survivors of severe head injury and, second, the introduction of the 1981 Education Act, which makes provision for the assessment of children with special educational needs. The residual language problems after head injury in childhood can cover a wide range and require comprehensive assessment if they are to be suitably managed. As Ylvisaker (1985) stated, in a discussion of the neuro-psychological sequelae of head injury in children, 'the traditional view that children are relatively impervious to the effects of acquired brain injury has obviously been overstated' as more and more evidence of the long-term effects of childhood head injury become available.

Natural history

There are three stages to the recovery of a head-injured child. The length of the stages is variable and probably depends on the severity of the injury.

1. The acute period lasts from emergency admission to the re-establish-ment of the stable conscious state. The trauma team will be at its most active during this period. Neurosurgery, various investigations and inten-sive care monitoring may all be a necessary part of the management. A small number of children may return to a situation of having wake–sleep cycles but unfortunately make no further progress. This is described as a 'persistent vegetative state'.
2. From the re-establishment of the stable conscious state a period of consistent recovery usually begins. This period may be very short in the mildly or moderately injured child, or may last for several months in a more severely injured child. It is a time for therapy and educational input to maximise recovery. Thorough and ongoing assessment needs to be carried out and a goal-oriented treatment programme used which aims towards functional rehabilitation. Where progress through this period is fast, the child may appear to regain the norm on a number of skills

quickly. This does not mean, however, that more long-term difficulties may not develop later, particularly when the child returns to school where learning may not be sustained.

3. Towards the end of this period, a slowing down of progress will be observed resulting in recovery appearing to plateau. At this stage, long-term residual deficits will become apparent. The time it takes for the child to reach this stage will again depend on the severity of the injury. Only consistent and comprehensive assessment will reveal whether progress is tailing off. Where there is a return more or less to the previous levels, at least in some skills, long-term residual problems may be overlooked. Where there are multiple persisting deficits, a consistent, specific and intensive approach to treatment is probably necessary.

To establish the short-term needs of these children, appropriate to the second stage of recovery, Ewing-Cobbs et al. (1985) looked at the language function of a group of children 5 months after childhood head injury. They found aphasic language problems in less than 10% of the sample and concluded that language difficulties after paediatric head injury were 'non-specific in nature, and did not vary consistently with the type of cerebral involvement'. The need for long-term follow-up was also emphasised, particularly as it had been suggested that problems in the later acquisition of language skills such as reading may be delayed following childhood head injury. This was previously suggested by Chadwick et al. (1981). Their study of the intellectual performance, scholastic achievement and reading skills of 97 children at least 2 years after head injury led them to conclude that 'brain injury is more likely to impair the acquisition of new skills than to cause the loss of well established old skills'. They noticed in particular that this was true for children under 5 years of age at the time of injury, with regard to their later acquisition of written language skills. This was an important finding that helped to dispel the old myth that brain injury in young children had few serious long-term consequences.

There is no consensus about the length of follow-up constituting a long-term study, and this is particularly relevant to children in the third stage. Jordan, Ozanne and Murdoch (1988) examined a group of 20 children aged 8–16 years who had sustained childhood head injury at least 12 months previously. They found that the language test scores of the head-injured group were be significantly lower than those of their control group. The performance of both groups on the Frenchay Dysarthria Test (Enderby, 1983) was well within the normal range, so they do not appear to have had motor speech problems, which can complicate the clinical presentation after head injury in childhood. They concluded that it was important to include both long- and short-term monitoring of language in this group.

Role of the speech and language therapist

Speech and language therapy intervention needs to begin with appropriate assessment and diagnosis. However, for the head-injured child with ACA there are several factors that can complicate this clinical task:

1. Traumatic brain injury, both localised and diffuse, is likely to give rise to a complex association of motor, cognitive, perceptual, emotional and communication problems.
2. There is little formal assessment material available which is specifically designed to meet the needs of these children.
3. The previous outline of the stages of recovery indicate that the deficits are likely to change from day to day, week to week or month to month, depending on the stage the child has reached.
4. Traumatic brain injury is still sufficiently uncommon to mean that most staff are relatively inexperienced in this area and that few specialists are available.

Reasssessment is clearly important for measuring recovery. As each individual child's response to brain injury will vary, the only way to know what stage the child is at and how to establish the next goal for intervention is to use an appropriate protocol. This is particularly necessary in the following circumstances:

1. During the second stage of recovery where the child's situation is changing rapidly and/or often so that intervention keeps up with these changes.
2. During the third stage of recovery where the situation is rather static in order to draw up a comprehensive profile of the child's specific deficits.
3. At any stage where therapy is being given, to evaluate its effect and redirect goals as necessary.
4. At any time when the child is said to have 'recovered' but is still experiencing difficulty at school, to see if any residual problems have been overlooked.

Informal assessment and screening procedures such as the Children's Aphasia Screening Test (Whurr and Evans, 1986) may be useful in the initial stages, particularly in young children. However, the mildly or moderately aphasic child soon reaches the ceiling on such tests and they rarely provide a sufficiently detailed profile for long-term use with the severely aphasic child. The choice of formal assessment will depend on the stage of recovery the child is at and the level of cooperation. It should be emphasised that developmental assessments such as the Reynell Development Language Scales (Reynell, 1985) are rarely able to describe the specific difficulties of this group. The battery of tests used in both clinical situations and research studies is outlined in Appendix I, although it does not claim to include all the tests that could be used with this group.

It is important to remember that language problems after head injury in childhood are likely to occur alongside speech production problems such as dysarthria and dyspraxia. More fundamental oral dysfunction problems are likely to dominate rehabilitation in the early stages. Where there is any doubt about the competence of the swallowing mechanism, an examination using videofluoroscopic radiology should always be carried out. The differential diagnosis of dysphasia and dysarthria, although theoretically straightforward, may be less so in practice. Although the primary concern here is language, some of the difficulties in managing motor speech problems need to be outlined briefly. The problems are similar to those encountered when assessing the children's language. With very little specific assessment material available the use of two types of assessments predominates:

1. The use of adult material. In this respect the Frenchay Dysarthria Test (Enderby, 1983) is most commonly used by speech and language therapists expressing a preference. However, it is difficult to use this test successfully with children under 8 years of age and almost impossible where they are uncooperative.
2. The use of informal material. Most therapists use their own informal assessments. These should include assessment of head position and general posture (in conjunction with a physiotherapist), the presence or absence of oral reflexes, the control of respiration and phonation, observation and movement of the facial musculature, dentition, swallowing and the control of saliva. The major problem in the use of informal assessments is in developing a scoring or recording scheme which allows the therapist to document the presenting situation and which allows for reliable reassessment measures.

The Paediatric Oral Skills Package (Brindley et al., 1993) has set out to do this. It aims to provide a profile of a child's oral skills and can be used with those aged between 0 and 16 years. There are three scales: observation, examination (for eating and drinking) and performance. Any combination of these can be chosen depending on the child's needs, age and ability to cooperate. The profile which is produced is then used as the basis upon which the clinician can formulate a hypothesis about the improvement of oral function for the individual child.

The problem of treatment is complicated by the fact that most head-injured children do not present with one 'pure' type of dysarthria. Usually the motor pattern is mixed and may include both upper and lower motor neuron signs. Most therapists initially become familiar with the assessment and treatment of oral motor problems in children through working with those having cerebral palsy. Although such experience is useful, the motor problems of head-injured children are different. This is both because of the mixed neurology arising from the diffuse cerebral damage and because of the acquired nature of the problem. The head-injured child, depending on the degree of recovery, has had a wealth of pre-traumatic experience. The way in which this is recalled by the child will vary, but must be a consideration when planning treatment. It is certainly different from the child with a congenital motor disorder who has no previous experience of unimpaired function. The presence of other problems, particularly in language and cognition, but also possibly sensorimotor, may make it difficult for the head-injured child to understand what is required during treatment. Models need to be clearly presented within a structured framework. Frequent repetition of the desired target is also required in order to accommodate these difficulties and the variable attention span which may also be a feature.

In the very earliest stages of recovery, the head-injured child may have no communication at all, or only be able to communicate non-verbally. To leave a child with severe communication difficulties, and the child's family without speech and language therapy support in the initial period of rapid recovery, even if you think the child will improve, is not appropriate. Informed and sensitive help with be required by both the child and the family if they are to cope with communication difficulties that are likely to arise. Alternative or augmentative communication may be appropriate in the immediate post-trauma period to ease communication problems. However, it is not a straightforward matter of supplying a communication aid and leaving the child, family and other staff to get on with it. The following considerations are important:

1. The child's reaction to sudden loss of communication and other skills: this has not been studied extensively but it is recognised that brain injury is a catastrophic insult which is likely to leave the child confused and fearful. After head injury in children, a condition of post-traumatic mutism has been commonly encountered. Levin et al. (1983) stated that mutism is more common after head injury in children than in adults. They gave an account of the recovery of a 12-year-old girl who was mute for 3 weeks post-trauma. It is not clear whether mutism is primarily related to the overall effect of the cerebral damage or whether it is a psychological reaction to loss of function. There have been varied reports concerning the length of the mute period. Hecaen (1976) reported a period of up to 21 days. It may affect all communication modalities or be specifically related to the use of verbal language. The child may or may not be interested in using an alternative communication device during this time.

2. The family may insist on 'normality' of approach: this is especially true where they equate alternative communication with the acceptance of handicap. The traumatic effect of the head injury is not related only to

the injury to the child's brain. The family too is 'injured' and will need to work through reactions of grief and loss. Coming to terms with the effect of the injury has been described by families as mourning for the child they have lost and getting to know the head-injured child as a new member of the family. This reaction probably relates to the considerable physical, cognitive and personality changes that can be the sequelae of severe head injury

3. The associated motor, visual and perceptual problems may limit the choice of system or device; although these problems are not insurmountable in the long term, assessment for such devices is probably best carried out at a specialist centre. The provision of computer hardware, software and switches is a complex area requiring the combined approached of an experienced multidisciplinary team. A number of national centres exist to advise about the provision of communication aids. However, in the short term, a less 'hi-tech' approach and the use of commonsense may be the best answer.

4. The underlying language and cognitive problems: these may mean that, where complex instructions are required, the child cannot understand how to use the device. Non-verbal demonstration is probably the best answer to this problem. Time spent just playing alongside the child and being with the family, seeing what fits their communication needs, is also essential.

5. The speed at which the problem changes: this may mean that the device is only appropriate for a short time and needs frequent changing or adjustment. This highlights the importance of regular reviews.

With regard to these points, the following methods are recommended, particularly in the early stages of recovery.

Gestural communication

This may be introduced informally and later developed into a more formal system if necessary. The framework of the Makaton Vocabulary (Walker, 1980) is recommended because it is adaptable, fairly simple, already known in many places, and training courses are readily available. Basic gestures/signs should be used consistently by all those working with the child, e.g. nurses, therapists, medical staff, teachers etc. It is usually helpful to ask the family to suggest the things they want to communicate to or with the child. Where possible the child's own suggestions should also be included. Some children will readily make up their own signs or use mime to communicate.

Communication boards

These should be tailored to the child's needs as much as possible. Personal photographs are often a good idea to stimulate interest, add a real element of communicative intent and aid recall. They may also help the family to become involved in the project. Although some ready-made boards are available, a multipurpose Perspex board, in which the pictures or symbols can be changed regularly, is often more flexible in keeping up with the child's changing needs. Avoid static pictures of uninteresting objects. Rather, choose life-like objects and actions within a contextual setting.

In the later stages of recovery, before any effective therapy programme can be implemented, the severity of the specific deficits should be carefully investigated. A goal-oriented approach which is regularly reviewed is recommended for the following reasons:

1. It can be graded in a step-like manner and should be based on the child's strengths and needs. Thus, when working through the range of auditory processing difficulties, for example, it is important to begin therapy in a distraction-free environment as far as auditory interference is concerned, where the child can function well. Then the approach can work up through various situations which the child may encounter with less ease, including those found at home and school, and both formal and informal in nature. Where possible try to use both individual and group situations.

2. When teaching syntax a structured approach is preferred. Both the Colour Pattern Scheme (Lea, 1970) and the Derbyshire Language Scheme (Knowles and Masidlover, 1982) are useful. For review of ways to use the Derbyshire Language Scheme, in both assessment and management of various age groups, see Lees and Urwin (1991).

3. A consistent approach to the use of cueing to aid confrontational naming and word finding allows the child to generalise these skills more readily. Experience suggests that the child may pass through different stages at which different types of cues aid recall. Work in adult aphasia (Howard, et al., 1985) has suggested that different types of cues may be effective over different time periods. Clinical experience suggests that children may use different cues even within the normal population (see Appendix I). Commonly the cues used early in recovery are gestural, with verbal description and phonemic cues developing as later strategies.

4. The child should be encouraged to develop a capacity for self-monitoring errors. For the long-term benefit of the brain-injured child, relearning a self-monitoring strategy is of the utmost importance, both for social independence and for educational placement. The use of video in small group sessions may be a helpful technique, particularly with teenagers in the later stages of recovery.

5. Long stretches of individual therapy in traditional treatment centres may not always be the most appropriate management for children and teenagers with long-term problems. The therapist needs to be as flexible as

possible when considering the place, timing and style of therapy offered and its effect on motivation.

Problems with written language can occur after head injury in children. Age at injury does appear to be one of the prognostic factors. Ewing-Cobbs et al. (1985) reported that head-injured children demonstrated greater difficulty with written language tests than head-injured adolescents, regardless of the severity of the injury. The few studies with this population have failed to establish the specific ways in which the processing of written language is broken down. Also they have not outlined the strategies used by head-injured children to overcome reading and spelling problems. These are two important considerations when therapists and teachers seek to plan remedial programmes. When seeing a head-injured child with reading and spelling problems, it is therefore important that comprehensive language assessment should be carried out to confirm that other difficulties really do not exist.

Children referred with persisting spelling problems frequently also have high level auditory comprehension problems, auditory discrimination problems and other difficulties with the discrimination and manipulation of phonemes, as well as word-finding problems, both general and specific. These high level language problems may have been overlooked because they can be difficult to measure in practice. A range of tests is available including the Neale Analysis of Reading Ability (Neale, 1958) and the Graded Word Spelling Test (Vernon, 1977). Where a more broadly based screening test is required the Aston Index (Newton and Thompson, 1976) could be used; designed for children aged 5–10 years it includes a vocabulary test, a draw-a-man test, a reading and a spelling test, as well as memory, sound discrimination and sound-blending tasks. Two profiles of the child's strengths and weaknesses in these skills can be drawn up from the results. It is a procedure that may be familiar to some teachers. Where possible, the speech and language therapist should seek to work alongside the teacher and psychologist whenever assessing a child with written language problems.

It is also important to make a thorough investigation of reading and spelling strategies used by the child. Most children do develop strategies for overcoming current difficulties, even if it is a negative strategy such as 'don't know'. Working with the child will reveal if any route is functional for the transposition of phonemes to graphemes (i.e. is the strategy predominantly based on visual memory, or is it phonetic?), what knowledge of errors the child has and what self-correction strategies, if any, are employed. It may be difficult to establish pre-trauma levels of language competence but it is important to look for any evidence of a family history of spelling difficulty or language problems. Clinical folklore abounds with stories about the numbers of head-injured children who were not very competent language users before injury or who came from a family of poor language users. This should not be taken as an indication that the child would have had some reading and writing difficulties anyway and that therefore nothing needs to be done. The combined effects of early developmental difficulty and further brain injury are likely to cause long-term problems and each child's needs must be individually assessed. The speech and language therapist and teacher should approach the management of written language difficulties together, providing an appropriate remedial programme which is aimed at the child's educational needs and future language competence.

Rehabilitation of head-injured children

It should be clear that traumatic brain injury can give rise to numerous potential difficulties for the child. Add to this the background of the child's continuing development and it becomes clear that for the child's full learning potential to be maximised rehabilitation is properly a multi-disciplinary concern. However, few rehabilitation centres exist to meet these needs. The child may be fortunate to spend the acute period in a children's ward of a specialist hospital where an acute rehabilitation team will implement an initial programme. Most often this will include physiotherapist, occupational therapist, psychologist, teacher, and speech and language therapist, alongside nursing and medical staff and the child's family. It will be important to begin to establish a daily routine for the child. The programme must be well understood by all concerned with carrying it out and reviewed regularly.

On discharge from hospital most of the 27 speech and language therapists responding to the 1986 questionnaire on the management of children with ACA said that between 60% and 100% of the children they had seen continued to need speech and language therapy. However, many children will return to minimal provision and few will go on to placement in a specialised centre; indeed, some will not even have begun to have their educational needs assessed at this stage. All too often, clinical experience has shown that it is only years later, perhaps when legal claims for compensation are being dealt with, that some of these fundamental needs will be identified for the first time.

Once a child has a statement of educational need, then placement is up to the local education authority. The availability of provision will vary but many children find themselves placed in schools for children with physical disabilites. Many of these schools, recognising the challenges of meeting the needs of this group, are now arranging for local in-service training for their staff to provide them with the information and skills needed to work with head-injured children. A small network of local support groups, under the guidance of the Children's Head Injury Trust,* is now growing.

* Neurosurgery, The Radcliffe Infirmary, Oxford OX2 6HE.

Two particular aspects of the rehabilitation needs of head-injured children will be considered here – neuropsychology and neuropsychiatry – as these are not available in all areas. Johnson and Roethig-Johnson (1987) addressed some of the psychological needs of head-injured children. In the classroom, they described the head-injured child as one who 'becomes increasingly worried or frightened without really understanding why' and who gradually falls behind classmates. This is the beginning of what they termed the 'backward slide away from the peer group academically and socially'. They reported studies which have suggested that head-injured children find tasks requiring increased speed particularly difficult in comparison to their peers. It is the child's ability to integrate complex information and attend to tasks in a range of modalities which will determine whether or not he or she experience the backward slide. The role of the neuropsychologist will include assessing the various component skills used in a range of cognitive tasks of different complexity.

It is also recognised that the increasing number of children surviving head injury has led to a growing need for neuropsychiatric services for this group (Parmelee and O'Shanick, 1987). A study by McCabe and Green (1987) is one of the few to date which has tried to understand the head-injured child's perspective. They reported three adolescents who had suffered severe head injury and who displayed socially disinhibited behaviours. By implementation of individually structured programmes, they were able to effect some behavioural maturation, especially preparation for independent living. They also discussed the needs of families who have to cope with head-injured adolescents. Understandably, they reported a tendency for parents to develop 'an overprotective and lenient approach whereby limit-setting and appropriate challenge of the young person becomes reduced'. McCabe and Green also discussed a number of components of a neuropsychiatric service to head-injured children which included: voluntary support systems, group psychotherapy, the appointment of a key worker, family support, the use of pharmacological therapies and, if necessary, the provision of secure hospital placement.

Examples of children with head injury

It is not unusual for claims that children with head injuries had developmental learning difficulties before their subsequent brain injury. This is always difficult to establish, unless the child had already had special educational needs identified. Case 6 is a child about whom such concerns had been voiced, but no specific provision made, prior to his injury.

Case 6

This boy had a history of a mild general developmental and language delay. All his early milestones had been achieved at the low end of the normal range; his first words were at 2 ½ years of age and he had one elder brother who attended a school for children with moderate learning difficulties. He sustained a severe closed head injury at the age of 5;3 years in a road traffic accident. He was admitted to hospital in an unconscious state. The right side responded to pain with flexion and the left with extension. He was given mannitol, intubated and ventilated, and transferred to a neurosurgical unit. His pupils were small and reacted sluggishly to light. There were lacerations to his arm and tongue which were sutured, and abrasions to the skull, shoulders and right hand. A CT scan at this time showed moderate cerebral oedema and no intra-cranial bleeding. Five days post-onset he began to have generalised seizures and these were treated with anticonvulsants. Ten days post-trauma he was breathing independently and he was taken off the ventilator. Gastroscopy revealed stomach erosions and an acute duodenal ulcer which was also treated appropriately.

A repeat CT scan 6 weeks post-onset showed a degree of cerebral atrophy and enlarged lateral ventricles. He remained mute for 5 months. His first utterances were coprolalic and this persisted for 1 month. At 6 months post-injury he was producing appropriate two-word phrases and some paraphasic errors (Table 3.1). Nine months post-injury an assessment of general cognitive abilities was said to indicate a moderate degree of learning difficulty. There was a residual spastic weakness affecting the legs and the left arm, con-tractures and deformities in the lower limbs. He had a moderate mixed dysphasia. His hearing was normal. An assessment of special educational needs was made and he was placed in a school for children with physical and learning difficulties.

Expressive language was non-fluent as these two examples recorded 1 year post-injury demonstrate.

Dog Story
'A dog ....who had meat..and he dropped it in the river.... and the other dog ate it.'

Conversation about a swimming trip (the interpretation in brackets was provided by his father):

'It was Barbara's seaside [i.e. near where she lived]. It was a different pool. It was a blue pool [i.e. swimming pool]. Can I go home now?'

It is clear that this child's expressive language was limited. However, the extent to which inherited factors or the brain injury he sustained contributed cannot be determined. All that can be said is that it has been observed that both genetic factors and brain injury can lead to a pattern of reduced language skill. The overall pattern of his language recovery post-injury is shown in Figure 3.1.

Table 3.1 Expressive language and naming errors during recovery for Case 6

Post-trauma (months)	Item	Response	Error type
8	Saucepan	Oven	Semantic paraphasia
9	Car	The car goes in the petrol	
12	Camel	Kangaroo	Semantic paraphasia
	Leaf	Flower	Semantic paraphasia
	Feather	Flower	Semantic paraphasia and perseveration
	Diver	Robot	Semantic paraphasia
16	Camel	Kangaroo/donkey	Semantic paraphasia
	Diver	Spaceman	Semantic paraphasia

Grammatical errors at the same assessment:

It's getting dark	It's coming on night time
It's a girl	It ain't a boy it's a her

The considerable number of variables that influence the outcome of head injury in childhood make it difficult to make specific predictions on the basis of, for example, age alone. Below, two girls (Cases 7 and 8) of about the same age who suffered head injury are reported to demonstrate some of the potential variability of outcome which is more likely to be related to severity and extent of damage, and to which the provision of different rehabilitation facilities may also have made a contribution.

Case 7

This girl (first reported by Lees and Urwin, 1991) had a normal developmental history until she was involved in a road traffic accident at the age of 12 years in which she sustained severe multiple injuries. She was admitted, unconscious, with a severe head injury, ruptured spleen and haemorrhage, pneumothorax and chest injury, and fractures of the right clavicle and ankle. A score on the Glasgow Coma Scale of 5 was recorded at this stage. A CT scan was reported to show subarachnoid blood over the right cerebellar hemisphere, within the vermis, the fourth ventricle and the right lateral ventricle. There were two dissociated intracerebral bleeds and virtually no oedema. This was described as a general cerebral contusion.

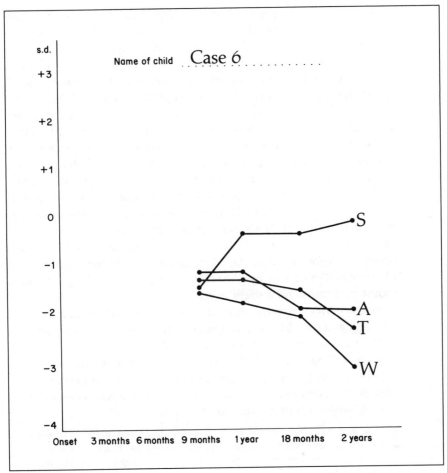

Figure 3.1 Profile of recovery of Case 6: A, auditory association; S, sentence repetition; T, TROG; W, Word Finding Vocabulary Test

As a result of her deteriorating condition a repeat scan was carried out 24 hours later. It was unchanged. However, a further scan 7 days later suggested that the haematomas were less dense, although there was little change in the size of the ventricles. She was nursed in intensive care for 4 weeks; for the first week she was critically ill. At this stage ultrasonic angiography showed no evidence of occlusion of the extracranial carotid arteries, and middle cerebral artery flow was detected to be the same bilaterally. However, there was a suggestion of increased and turbulent flow in the left jugular and possible obstruction in the right jugular artery.

After leaving the critical care stage she had evidence of a very severe motor disorder. There was spasticity in the right limbs and extrapyramidal signs on the left side including tremor. Six weeks post-trauma she began to show some awareness of her surroundings. At 10 weeks post-injury she was responding to being spoken to but had a severe repetitive and expressive dysphasia. She had a profound motor disorder. Twelve weeks post-injury she was making steady progress and marked improvement was noted in all skills; she was responsive, cooperative, cheerful and talking. There had been a great improvement in motor function. The right side was still worse than the left, but she had reasonable hand function on both sides, could sit independently and walk with support. She continued to make excellent progress and was discharged to a weekly boarding placement for rehabilitation, where she gained mobility to walk independently within 1 year. She continued to make good progress with language and learning, within this structured environment. Both education and therapy were well integrated, goal oriented and directed to specific deficits. Two years post-trauma she was transferred to another school for children with physical difficulties nearer her home, with only moderate residual motor problems and a slight dysarthria.

Assessment of naming difficulties on the Word Finding Vocabulary Test and the Graded Naming Test shows the types and range of naming errors during her recovery (Table 3.2).

Story telling showed the generally non-fluent nature of her expressive language: frequent hesitations, some repetitions and false starts. The overall content of the story was well preserved.

Dog Story recorded 6 months post onset:

> 'The dog had a piece of meat he was taking home and on his way he had to cross a plank over....over a pond. He looked down and .... there was ..... his own reflection in the water and he thought there.... in the water was another dog...with the piece of meat. He thought he'd have that piece of meat too .... So he snatched at the dog .... but as he opened his mouth.... the piece of meat fell into the pond and was never seen again.'

Case 8

This girl (first reported by Lees and Urwin, 1991) had a normal developmental history. She was from a bilingual Italian/English family. She was admitted to hospital at the age of 11;6 years in an unconscious state, having been knocked down by a car on her way to school. She was unresponsive and her pupils were small. An emergency CT scan showed multiple contusions in the left anterior and the right posterior parts of the internal capsule, with possible blood in the right lateral ventricle. She had a displaced fracture of the right tibia. She was admitted to the intensive care unit, ventilated and given intravenous mannitol. The EEG was not abnormal.

Table 3.2   Assessment of naming difficulties on the Word Finding Vocabulary Test and the Graded Naming Test during recovery of Case 7

Initial assessment	Item	Response	Error types
2 months post-trauma	Cup	Cup	
	Table	Table	
	Boat	Sink	Semantic paraphasia
	Tree	Glass	Semantic paraphasia
	Window	Table	Semantic paraphasia
	Snake	Table	Perseveration
	Basket	Table	Perseveration
	Saw	Knife	Semantic paraphasia
	Clown	Dog	Semantic paraphasia
	Bear	Dog	Perseveration
	Moon	Pear	Semantic paraphasia
	Chimney	Chair	Semantic paraphasia
9 months post-onset	Lighthouse	Windmill/ lightmill/ lighthouse	Self-corrected Semantic paraphasia
2 years post-onset	Buoy	Sandcastle	Semantic paraphasia
	Corkscrew	Screwdriver	Semantic paraphasia
	Turtle	Tortoise	Semantic paraphasia

Brain-stem and visual evoked responses showed increased latency. She was ventilated for 13 days, during which time she did not respond to commands and had marked dystonic movements, more on the left than on the right.

She remained unchanged for 5 weeks when she suddenly started responding to commands and became less restless. She was mobile, could understand simple requests, had single word speech, and was eating and drinking well. She also regained continence of urine and faeces within the same week. She was discharged 6 weeks later with a mild, right upper motor neuron, seventh nerve palsy, a tremor of the left hand which was worse on movement, a slightly broad-based gait and a moderate mixed dysphasia.

She returned to her previous mainstream secondary school but had considerable problems in language, learning and emotional stability. Within the large, mixed ability classes, in which it was difficult to give specific teaching help, she made very poor progress and became depressed. It was difficult for the family to attend local speech and language therapy appointments, even in the school holidays, and she therefore received little specific help. She had a dysphonia due to bilateral vocal fold weakness and a significant word-finding problem. Two years post-trauma, a statement of educational needs was eventually made by which she received extra teaching help of 0.2 w.t.e. (whole time equivalent, i.e. amount of support given for a child). She received some outpatient treatment from a department of child and adolescent psychiatry. She said she had few friends, felt isolated and found it difficult to communicate with her parents. Her responses on the Graded Naming Test (McKenna and Warrington, 1983) showed some of the naming difficulties she had (Table 3.3).

Table 3.3 Assessment of naming difficulties on the Word Finding Vocabulary Test and the Graded Naming Test during recovery of Case 8

Post-trauma	Item	Response	Error type
3 months	Camel	Giraffe	Semantic paraphasia
	Goat	Giraffe	Perseveration
	Waterfall	Waterchute	Semantic paraphasia
9 months	Cup	Glass	Semantic paraphasia
2½ years	Kangaroo	Giraffe	Semantic paraphasia
5 years	Buoy	Tambourine	Semantic paraphasia
	Thimble	Nimble	Phonemic paraphasia

Her progress with story telling showed that she gradually became more fluent and was able to use longer sentences. These examples are from the Dog story, the first one at 6 months post-onset:

'There was a dog walking with a piece of meat in his mouth .... He saw another dog ..... with another piece of meat in his mouth. The meat fell out of his mouth.'

Then again at 18 months post-onset:

'The dog was walking home with a piece of meat in his mouth .... and he crossed a plank.... and then saw a river and then saw his own reflection in the water and he thought it was another dog with another piece of meat in his mouth .... and... and so er.... he.. he dropped the meat and it fell in the river and he never saw it again.'

This written language sample revealed some of her feelings about her school placement and lack of friends. She complained of headaches and tiredness (common features of depression), and her description of her comprehension difficulties was consistent with her test results. The difficulties she had with her written language include spelling and punctuation errors, as well as some sentence formulation difficulties. This piece was written 1 year post-injury.

> teachers sort of miss me in class, I have tried to ask to play but all of a sudden they give lies meant to hurt me. When I stay with Friend I (fel) stay happier to them and they think twice. When I'm in class and the teacher goes to Fast For me and I get mygrians and because of that I move about a lot and do the work wrong somet(h)imes. Work sheets I have to read over again and again until I get aroond to now what its (an) about. everyBody had a Friend to(e) go home with play with and do over things with. if it carrys on like this I with just (t go hom) leave. [Self corrections in brackets; spelling and punctuation as original.]

She left home at the age of 17 years to live with close relatives and was given a place on a youth training scheme. However, she found time keeping difficult and was often late, or failed to attend at all. After a further period of psychiatric treatment she took up a place on another scheme, as a trainee receptionist, and coped better. She recognised that she had continued difficulty with communication and said herself 'I want to talk faster but it takes hours to come out, if I'm in a conversation it takes hours to get it out'. She was particularly mindful of the reactions of others to her word-finding problems. As she said 'People think you're stupid. I change the subject but it doesn't always work and it won't stop people thinking I'm stupid'. Her hobbies included a particular interest in personal fitness in order to make the best of her disability. All in all her reactions to her head injury are best summed up in her own words: 'I just feel like I missed a big gap in my life.'

The graphs of Figures 3.2 and 3.3 show the progress made by these two girls over the first 2 years following their head injuries. Clearly, Case 7 made significantly better progress overall than Case 8. All the scores for the former child (Case 7) were within the normal range by the end of the first year. Case 8 continued to have z-scores in the range -1 to -2, and below, at 2 years post-trauma, which directly reflected the moderate-to-severe nature of her aphasia and reported significant problems 5 years post-trauma. In both cases the most consistent period of progress was during the first 6 months following injury, after which progress gradually tailed off.

Conclusions about head injury

Not all children who suffer severe head injury will have severe residual aphasia or other communication difficulties. However, a complex range of speech and language problems makes up the common sequelae to severe brain injury along with other motor, cognitive and psychiatric problems. These are best dealt with by a multidisciplinary team within a rehabilitation

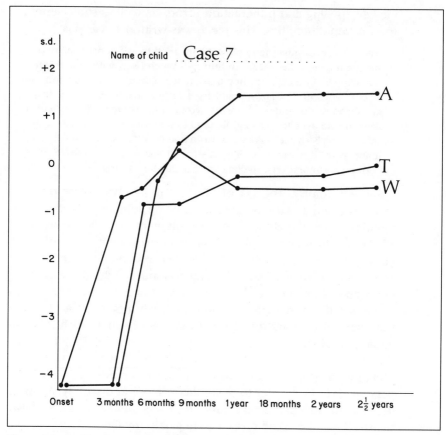

Figure 3.2 Profile of recovery of Case 7: A, auditory association; T, TROG; W, Word Finding Vocabulary Test

situation. Only comprehensive assessment carried out over time will reveal the nature of the child's changing needs and allow the appropriate management to be planned. There has been little attempt, to date, to document the effects of rehabilitation for head-injured children in sufficient detail for firm conclusions to be drawn. This requires urgent attention if we are to plan for the needs of this increasingly large population. Detailed case studies of children placed in rehabilitation programmes would contribute to the present lack of information in this area.

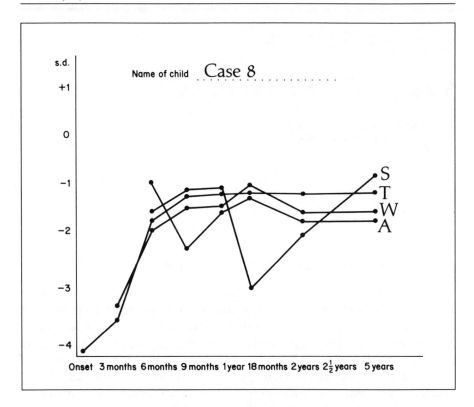

Figure 3.3 Profile of recovery of Case 8: A, auditory association; S, sentence repetition; T, TROG; W, Word Finding Vocabulary Test

Chapter 4
Other traumatic aphasias

Pathology and natural history

The major causes of traumatic aphasias in childhood are cerebrovascular lesions and head injury. However, a number of other smaller aetiological groups, some of which are not strictly traumatic but would be described as invasive are usually classified with the traumatic aphasias. Their aetiology is traumatic in the sense that there is some injury or invasion of the cerebral matter either by bacterial or viral agents or by neoplasm. Two other fringe problems, cerebral anoxia and comas of traumatic origin (i.e. not due to convulsive status), will also be considered with this group. It is recognised that coma is a result of trauma rather than a cause of aphasia, but the long-term recovery of children who have been in prolonged coma is of concern to professionals who see children with acquired disorders and is therefore included here.

Childhood infectious diseases of the central nervous system (CNS) are summarised by Smyth, Ozanne and Woodhouse (1990) and include meningitis, encephalitis and meningoencephalitis (where both the meninges and the brain are infected). These infections usually have a diffuse effect but focal infections do also occur.

Meningitis

Meningitis is an infection of the meninges usually involving the subarachnoid space and the cerebrospinal fluid; the infections are commonly bacterial in origin although viral meningitis infections can occur. Accurate diagnosis will require exmination and culture of the cerebrospinal fluid (CSF). There are three ways in which these infections spread to the meninges: from the extension of a pre-existing infection, usually of the sinuses or mastoid; from infection through the blood stream; or after fracture of the skull. One variable in determining the prognosis is the effectiveness of the antibiotics used against the infection. In general these have greatly reduced the mortality rate among children with cerebral infections. However, serve deficits of speech and language do still occur as can deafness, cerebral palsy and learning difficulties.

Cerebral abscess

Of the types of cerebral infection that can result in language impairment, intracranial abscess resulting in a focal lesion of the cortex of the left hemisphere is the most common. In early studies of ACA (Guttman, 1942; Collignon, Hecaen and Angelergues, 1968), children with aphasia after cerebral abscess, particularly of the left temporal lobe, were common. These usually arose as a complication of severe otitis media and mastoiditis (infection of the mastoid bone). They would then infect the middle to posterior portion of the temporal lobe. They are less common with the current use of antibiotics to treat otitis media.

Another area that is vulnerable to infection is the frontal lobes. Here an abscess may follow frontal sinusitis. Where the dominant hemisphere is involved, aphasia can be part of the presenting symptoms. Treatment usually involves surgical drainage of the abscess and antibiotics for the infection. Cerebral abscess has not been a frequent contributor to cases of aphasia in recent series, although one of the five cases reported by Lees and Neville (1990) did present in this way. There was no evidence of more than cortical damage in this case and the patient had a mild aphasia.

Encephalitis

Encephalitis is the common name for viral infection of the brain. The number of viruses which are known to attack the central nervous system is large. They may be transmitted in a number of ways: by human contact, by insects or by other animal contacts. Diagnosis will usually involve examin-ation of the CSF. Mortality and morbidity are common sequelae. Commonly, incomplete recovery results in a range of motor, sensory and cognitive deficits, ranging from mild to severe.

Cerebral tumours

Neoplasm is defined as abnormal new growth of tissue which may be benign or malignant. 'Intracranial tumour' and 'cerebral tumour' are the terms used to cover these space-occupying lesions of the brain. They may arise from the abnormal and increased division of a number of different cell types, which accounts for the variety of locations and the range of prog-noses. Regarding cerebral tumours as a cause of ACA, there are only a few detailed reports of specific cases in the literature.

Martins, Ferro and Trindale (1987) reported a case of what they termed 'acquired crossed aphasia in a child'. This was a 15-year-old right-handed boy who was diagnosed as having a right hemispheric tumour, the localisation of which was confirmed by CT scan and surgery. The tumour did not extend into the left hemisphere or involve the corpus callosum. He was severely aphasic and subsequently developed left focal seizures. Subsequent investigations, as the aphasia worsened, showed continued growth of the tumour and the child died 3 months after the initial diagnosis. As the boy was right-handed and all the cerebral damage was confined to the right hemisphere, they concluded that he had a crossed aphasia. He was only the second example of a child with a crossed aphasia in their larger series of 31 cases.

Another child with aphasia due to a cerebral tumour was described by Agostini and Kremin (1986). This boy had a slowly developing tumour, the exact location of which was not given; he was followed up for 3 years, during which time it was possible to monitor his language. His expressive language was said to have reduced progressively but his verbal comprehension remained unaffected. He was described as anomic and the overall pattern was said to be a transcortical motor aphasia. Of the two cases described by Paquier and Van Dongen (1991), one had a space-occupying lesion of the left temporoparietal area which was removed surgically. Later she developed a seizure disorder that was predominantly right-sided, was aphasic, and had a slight right hemiplegia and a right homonymous hemianopia. This 9-year-old girl demonstrated mild receptive comprehension deficits on the Token Test and a severe jargon aphasia with neologisms, paraphasia and perseverations. The aphasia did show some improvement but was still evident as a mild disturbance 2 years later, and the epilepsy also persisted.

According to Hudson (1990), posterior fossa tumours are prevalent in childhood. The implications of tumours of the cerebellum, fourth ventricle and brain stem for speech and language disorders in childhood has been considered by Hudson and colleagues (Hudson, Murdoch and Ozanne 1989; Hudson, 1990). Although ataxic dysarthria has been reported in children, these authors also draw attention to ongoing language problems in children following treatment for posterior fossa tumours. Mutism has also been described as a common postoperative symptom and this may last for several weeks. When it occurs it is said to indicate a poor speech prognosis. Hudson, Murdoch and Ozanne (1989) used the Frenchay Dysarthria Test to assess six children and found a wide range of motor speech problems. The retention of phonological immaturities was also observed in two of the children. The authors proposed a link between the occurrence of long-term language disabilities and post-surgical radiotherapy. Language impairments were observed in four of the six children presented. The only two children not to have language problems had not received post-surgical radiotherapy.

They concluded that 'although it is recognised that radiotherapy may be essential for the long term survival of the children ... the medical team needs to be aware of the possible long term effects that this treatment may have on language abilities'.

Cerebral anoxia

Normal brain function depends on receipt of an adequate and continuous supply of oxygen. Anoxia is defined as a condition in which the oxygen level in the body tissues falls below the level required to maintain normal function, and may be caused by a complete absence or deficiency of oxygen. There are two factors that regulate the supply of oxygen to the brain: the cerebral blood flow and the oxygen content of the blood. Cerebral anoxia may result from a drop in cerebral blood flow or from a drop in blood oxygen level, which can have a number of causes, including near-drowning and suffocation in addition to cardiac and respiratory arrest. The results of cerebral anoxia will depend, to a large extent, on the time of reduced oxygen level. Deficits may range from mild to severe and, in extreme cases, death can be the result. Where oxygen levels are restored to normal within 1-2 minutes, then there is unlikely to be any long-term effects.

Murdoch and Ozanne (1990) reviewed the literature on cerebral anoxia in children and subsequent speech and language deficits. They stated that both the grey and the white matter of the brain may be damaged in cerebral anoxia, and that anoxic lesions of the cerebral cortex are usually bilateral, although they may be asymmetrical. Equally, damage to the cerebellum was reported as a common finding in all types of cerebral anoxia. Regarding the brain-stem nuclei, they reported that damage here has been recorded as more severe in children than in adults.

There are only a few specific reports of children presenting with speech and language deficits subsequent to cerebral anoxia. Murdoch and Ozanne (1990) reviewed two papers that discussed a total of five children, one of whom continued to have major learning difficulties 5 years after the trauma, and four others with subcortical lesions who had reading problems (Aram et al., 1983; Aram, Ekelman and Gillespie, 1989). A number of other language symptoms, reported by Aram, Ekelman and Gillespie (1989), included auditory comprehension, word retrieval and expressive syntax problems. Slow articulation and poor verbal memory were also reported in one child. Murdoch and Ozanne (1990) concluded that children where at risk of potential acute and chronic speech and language problems following anoxic episodes in childhood. As with all types of ACA, the deficits may be subtle; only comprehensive assessment will reveal their true nature and extent to allow for planning of appropriate remediation.

Prolonged coma in childhood

There are a number of causes of coma in childhood, including traumatic brain injury, infectious diseases of the CNS and cerebral anoxia. A child may also fall into a coma as a result of prolonged convulsive status, but this group is considered in Chapter 6. Long-term recovery of children after coma has been poorly documented. Few studies have used adequate measures of cognitive and language skills and compared these with information available during the acute stage; therefore it is difficult to discuss prognosis for recovery after prolonged coma (coma of more than 24 hours' duration) in childhood. In practical terms, the satisfactory educational placement of survivors of childhood coma requires a comprehensive understanding of the child's cognitive and language skills.

A study by Kirkham, Edwards and Lees (1990) aimed to assess what proportion of children who survived prolonged coma consequently had cognitive and/or language deficits (either permanent or transient), motor problems, psychiatric problems and other neurological deficits. They also wished to establish whether there were any factors that were predictive of outcome, including the severity of the coma, its aetiology and the age of the child at the time of insult, in addition to some of the measures taken in the acute stage including cerebral perfusion pressure. The ultimate aim of the study was to define useful predictors of long-term cognitive–linguistic outcome during the acute stage.

A 5-year retrospective study of childhood survivors of coma was described. Thirty-five children (aged between 4 and 16 years at the time of testing) participated in the study. They were designated to one of three groups, depending on the severity of their coma, which was assessed by its length in days. The first group included children who were in a coma for 1 day or less; the second group included those in a coma for more than 1 day, but for less than or equal to 1 week; those in the third group were in a coma for over a week but for less than 60 days. The aetiology of the coma in these groups included cardiac arrest, encephalitis, head injury and other traumatic causes.

All of the children were in intensive care units during the coma, and measures of cerebral perfusion pressure and intracranial pressure were available in relation to the length and depth of the coma as well as to the outcome. Individual psychometric assessment was carried out on all the children up to 5 years after the end of the coma period using the tests listed:

1. The Wechsler Intelligence Scales for Children or the Griffiths Scale of Mental Ability (depending on age).
2. Neale Analysis of Reading and Vernon Graded World Spelling Test for those of school age.

3. The Test for Reception of Grammar for verbal comprehension of language.
4. Measures of memory, behaviour problems and motor impairment.

Results indicated a significant relationship between severity of coma and cognitive performance, between aetiology of coma and coma length, and between clinical measures of cerebral perfusion pressure etc. and cognitive ability (all significant at the 0.01 or 0.02 level) (Table 4.1). Therefore, the lower the cerebral perfusion pressure in the acute stage, the greater the likelihood of learning, motor and language difficulties. A trend was also observed between length of coma and motor ability, which was significant at the 5% level.

Table 4.1 Results from Kirkham, Edwards and Lees (1990) for 34 children surviving coma

---

Learning difficulties
  57% of children who survived coma were experiencing learning difficulties 5 years later (full-scale IQ less than 80)
  31% of these had severe learning difficulties

Special education
  42.5% of the children had special educational needs (1981 Education Act)
  34% of these attended special schools
  25% were in residential care (at least during the week)
  8.5% were receiving special help within mainstream education
  A further 8.5% were referred to an educational psychologist as a direct result of this study

Other problems
  57% of the children had motor difficulties
  34% of the children had epilepsy
  Two children had been referred for help with behavioural problems

---

Kirkham, Edwards and Lees (1990) concluded that cerebral perfusion pressure is a useful predictor of potential recovery from coma in childhood. Children who survive prolonged coma in childhood require detailed assessment of cognitive and language skills to plan for their educational needs, because a significant proportion of the children had special educational needs as a result of cognitive and language problems. In the view of Kirkham et al. this indicated the need for future larger, probably multi-centre, multidisciplinary studies to validate their findings. In addition the learning potential of children who have survived coma and their response to intervention need to be studied so that effective education and therapy can be planned for them.

Role of the speech and language therapist

Because of the possible co-presentation of speech and language disorders in these conditions, as well as other general learning and motor difficulties, the speech and language therapist needs to carry out comprehensive assessment of both speech and language skills. A number of tests have already been mentioned. As a minimum, verbal comprehension and expressive language, both naming and spontaneous language, should be tested. As far as motor speech disorders are concerned a few studies have used the Frenchay Dysarthria Test (Enderby, 1983). This is actually designed for use with adults but may be used with cooperative children over the age of about 8 years. The *Paediatric Oral Skills Package* (Brindley et al., 1993) should provide an assessment that is more appropriate to the needs of children. It includes three different scales: observation, examination and performance. The former is particularly useful for young children, and for those who are very ill or uncooperative. The examination scale is predominantly concerned with eating and drinking, and the performance scale with speech production and voluntary oral movements. The completed profile aims to assist therapists to set achievable goals in treatment planning for children with oral dysfunction.

Hudson (1990) concluded that the speech and language therapist should take an active role in the management of children treated for brain tumours, in both the long and short term 'even if intervention is not initially warranted or has been discontinued'. This advice could be generalised to all of the groups presented here. The results of Kirkham, Edwards and Lees (1990) confirmed that without long-term follow-up, children with special needs, for both language and general learning, may fail to be identified. It is important to use a suitable language protocol as described in Appendix I and to arrange to review the child at sensible intervals which may be monthly, 6-monthly or annually depending on the situation. In general, where the clinical picture is changing fast then more frequent review is indicated.

Where a child's speech and language needs have been recognised, then any decisions about intervention will depend on a number of variables, such as age, medical prognosis and educational provision. It is possible that augmentative or alternative communication techniques will be needed by some children, both those with general motor problems and those with deteriorating conditions. Where a local specialist in this aspect of management is not available then referral to a communication aids centre is advised.

Other aspects of the management of these aphasias

One of the reported sequelae of some types of meningitis, and occasionally of other cerebral infections, in childhood is hearing loss. Smyth, Ozanne and Woodhouse (1990) summarised more than a dozen infections known to cause hearing loss in childhood. They also discussed the recent changes in diagnostic audiology which has improved the detection of hearing loss in these children, especially the increased use of auditory brain-stem responses. All children who present with acquired aphasia should have a hearing test to establish audiological status. The competence of the auditory mechanism for effective language rehabilitation is equally important for children with developmental or acquired conditions.

Reported recovery of hearing loss associated with cerebral infection in children is also discussed by Smyth, Ozanne and Woodhouse (1990). They stated that 'there appears to be no doubt that in some instances recovery (either complete or partial) of auditory function can occur following even profound hearing loss' and went on to say that such recovery can occur over a long time scale throughout childhood. The study by Brookhouser, Auslareler and Meskan (1988), who reported 31% of a group of 280 children having sensorineural hearing loss after meningitis, also documented changes in hearing threshold in some of these children over the 3 ½ years of their study.

From reviews of this group of conditions, it is clear that any child could have a wide range of needs: motor, cognitive, sensory and social, as well as communication. The speech and language therapist working with the multiply handicapped child needs to give particular attention to effective team working. She or he will need to liaise with a number of medical, educational and social services professionals as well as the family. These professionals may change at various times during the course of the child's problems, as a result of the changing emphasis of the deficits in the acute or chronic stages. In the acute stage, it is important that all the rehabilitation personnel meet to set goals which all members of the team understand, especially the nursing staff and parents who will probably be managing the child most of the time. Instructions for other staff should be discussed beforehand and demonstrated in front of a therapist: the therapist observes another carrying out the instructions to check for accuracy. When written down, any instructions should be clear and simple. Diagrams should be provided where possible, or better still photographs. A Polaroid camera can do this quite cheaply and the photographs can be kept by the child's bed, together with the care plan, for everyone to refer to. This technique can be used for general motor activities such as posture and seating, for the use of a communication device or a feeding programme.

Examples of children with traumatic aphasias

Case 9: A child with a cerebral abscess

This boy (first described by Lees and Neville, 1990) presented with acute aphasia at 15 years of age, and a previous history of normal development. A CT scan revealed frontal cortical damage following the anteromedial frontal lobe and laterally round to the centro-sylvian region (i.e. involving the parietal lobe), secondary to a subdural abscess which was drained. There was no infarct and the damage would appear to have been purely cortical. Pure-tone audiometry confirmed normal hearing. The child's IQ before the illness had been measured for educational placement (at age 11 years) and said to be above average on the WISC. This would appear to have been preserved because he returned to continue his education at the same school and achieved 11 passes at GCE 'O' level at the usual time. He received a period of speech and language therapy for 3 months, starting 6 months post-onset. At that time he was experiencing considerable difficulty in initiating some sounds and had a dysfluent speech pattern. However, this improved during the course of therapy and was more or less unnoticeable 1 year post-onset. He never had a significant comprehension problem and he did not produce paraphasias. Once the initial dysfluency problem was overcome, his language soon returned to its former level, as shown by this example of the Farmer Story recorded 6 months post-onset:

> 'There once was a farmer, who owned a stubborn donkey. The farmer wanted to get the donkey into the barn. First he pushed him, then he pulled him, but the donkey would not move. So he asked the dog to bark so he could frighten the donkey into the barn, but the lazy dog refused. So he asked the cat to make it bark. The cat was cooperative and scratched the dog. The dog barked and the barking frightened the donkey so that he jumped into the barn.'

Figure 4.1 is a graph showing his recovery.

Case 10: A child with meningitis

This girl had a history of normal development until the age of 15;7 years when she was admitted in a coma. She had had a fever for a few days and this had been followed by severe headache, vomiting and drowsiness. A diagnosis of meningococcal meningitis was confirmed by exmination of the CSF. She was treated with penicillin and chloramphenicol for 10 days. On examination, there was a

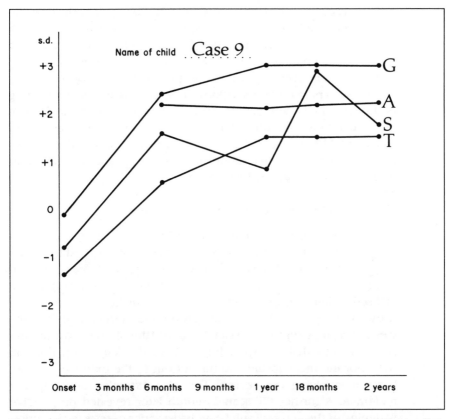

Figure 4.1 Profile of recovery of Case 9: A, auditory association; G, Graded Naming Test; T, TROG; W, Word Finding Vocabulary Test

right-sided motor disorder and problems with both comprehension and expressive language. There was a papilloedema, on the right more than on the left, minimal right-sided weakness of the face and arm, and a high-tone bilateral hearing loss of 45 dB.

One week post-onset, her TROG raw score was nine blocks passed (a z-score of -6) and her sentence repetition score was 5 (a z-score of -7.4). Expressive language at the same stage revealed both naming and grammatical errors. She produced 'yes' and 'no' responses appropriately, as well as some single word paraphasias (for example: brother = 'boyfriend' and tinopener = 'cantin'). Perseveration was also observed, particularly with the word 'oranges' being used as a persistent verbal error response. Grammar was telegrammatic, omitting prepositions and determiners so that only the main objects in action pictures were described, e.g. a man drinking was described as 'man and cup'. She had a tendency to reverse passive sentences to make them active and made errors with personal pronouns.

Two weeks post-onset she was still omitting main verbs or using incorrect verbs in short sentences, often making errors with verb endings or the pronouns. Word order difficulties were also observed including reversal (for example: 'the girl is giving the dog a bone' was described as 'the girl is give the bone a dog').

A CT scan performed 5 weeks post-onset showed some widening of the sulci on the left, in the parietal region only, and no abnormality of cerebral substance. She had a mild, residual, right facial weakness. She was almost at school-leaving age at the time of her illness and chose to leave school at the first opportunity. She found employment as a trainee hairdresser.

Case 11: a child with a viral encephalopathy

This girl had a normal developmental history until the age of 6 years when she presented with an obscure illness characterised by vomiting and generalised fever, followed by neck stiffness and an increase in tone. An EEG performed at the time showed a generalised, high-voltage, slow-activity abnormality, but no focal features. An initial CT scan and carotid and vertebral angiograms were normal. A repeat CT scan 1 month later showed low attenuation in both thalami, spreading out on the left to involve the posterior internal capsule and further out to the external capsule, but not involving the cortex. This also extended down to the mid-brain. A further CT scan 1 month later revealed progressive widening of the cerebral sulci. She had a series of tests for infection and metabolic abnormalities without any specific diagnosis being made. On the premise that she might have non-specific cerebritis she was started on a course of steroids and thereafter made a steady improvement. Pure-tone audiometry confirmed normal hearing. She continued on steroids for 1 year, over which period she appeared to make an excellent recovery. Three years later her Full-scale IQ (WISC-R) was 92, with Verbal IQ at 98 and Performance IQ at 88.

Although her general level of ability was within the normal range she continued to find it difficult to learn in mainstream school and made slow progress, particularly with reading. At the age of 8;1 years, her Neale Analysis of Reading Ability was an age equivalent of 8;0 years for accuracy, but 7;3 years for comprehension. Samples of written language produced 20 months post-onset show some of her difficulties (self-corrected errors are in brackets):

'The dog tried to chasing the cat and the cat tried to chasing the dog and wad day the cat and dog sed to each other lets be[e] friends.'

'It was snowing before going to school and it was very cold out side because was [ter] snowing and after lunch we[v] coom home and it was time to amegng the birds wes seeds and bread and cheese.

Expressive language samples during recovery using the Farmer Story show some mild difficulties:

Fifteen months post-onset:

'There was a farmer. The farmer wanted to put the donkey in the barn. First he pushed him but it was still. Then he pulled him but it did not move. So he asked the dog to woof at the donkey. But he stayed still. So he asked the cat to scratch him. The cat scratched him. The dog started woofing. The donkey was frightened and ran in the barn.'

Thirty-four months post-onset:

'There was a donkey, a very very naughty donkey. One day the farmer wanted the donkey to go in the barn. First of all he pushed him. Then he pulled him and he didn't.... and the lazy donkey fused to move. So then he asked the dog to bark at the..at the.. at the donkey. But he didn't fuse so he got the cat to scratch the dog. The cat scratched the dog. The dog barked and made the donkey go in the barn.'

Forty-four months post-onset:

'There was a.. a lazy donkey who w..who wouldn't go into the barn. The farmer tried to push the donkey but then he tried to pull him into the barn. He tried to ask the cat (hesitation) the dog to bark at the.... bark at the donkey but the dog didn't want to. So instead he asked the cat to scratch the dog which might frighten the donkey in to the barn. So the cat /srækt/ scratched the dog and the dog barked at the donkey and then the um... donkey jumped into the barn.'

Conclusions

In such a varied group as presented in this chapter, there can be few general conclusions. Once again a number of variables seem to be operating and, without larger studies, probably using pooled data, it is difficult to determine how they interact. However, there are a number of guidelines which can be used in the management of these children:

1. Older children will not necessarily have more severe or longer-term problems than younger ones. Check the severity of the aphasia over time and do not forget to follow up younger children beyond the age of learning written language to see if this has been affected.
2. Where the child has a history of coma of more than 24 hours duration be aware that an assessment of special educational needs may be indicated.

The importance of comprehensive assessment and multidisciplinary working must again be emphasised. We need to learn much more about the short-term and long-term effects on speech and language in all of these subgroups. We also need more detailed description of the rehabilitation programmes which may benefit these children. An area that has attracted very little consideration is the construction of curricula specific to children with multiple needs. As for the medical sequelae of this group, obviously cerebral tumour may have a poor prognosis, depending on the malignancy and the remission rate. In young children, where survival after a tumour appears to be good, language development may still be affected by treatment used to control the malignancy, including radio- and chemo-therapy. In children with multiple needs, where severe and uncontrolled epilepsy is a sequela, the prognosis is also likely to be reduced further.

Part II
Convulsive Aphasias

Chapter 5
Landau–Kleffner syndrome

Pathology

The Landau–Kleffner syndrome must be the most puzzling language disorder of childhood. It is probably the rarest, and many paediatric speech and language therapists will never have seen a case. First described by Landau and Kleffner in 1957, it has a number of other names. It is also called acquired aphasia with convulsive disorder and acquired receptive aphasia. These names refer to the co-occurring neurological disorder and the predominantly receptive language difficulty. There has been some confusion with the Worster-Drought syndrome, after Worster-Drought described a series of cases with what he called 'an unusual form of acquired aphasia in childhood' (Worster-Drought, 1971). These are taken to be examples of convulsive aphasia of the Landau–Kleffner type rather than the condition which is usually referred to as Worster-Drought syndrome; the latter is a motor speech disorder also called congenital suprabulbar paresis (Worster-Drought, 1956).

In general terms, the pattern of presentation in the Landau–Kleffner syndrome is that language regresses after a period of normal language development, usually with an accompanying seizure disorder. Beaumanoir (1985) described the two major symptoms as 'an acquired aphasia and a paroxysmal electroencephalographic recording with spikes and spikes and waves, mostly multifocal and unstable in the course of evolution', which may be associated with behaviour disturbances and epilepsy. The pathological basis of the disorder is not known, although numerous hypotheses have been advanced. These have been summarised by Dulac, Billard and Arthius (1983); first, the '*hypothese lesionelle*' (lesional hypothesis), which suggests that the EEG abnormalities and the language problems are the product of the same pathology – an inflammatory process in the cortex. Cerebral biopsies have failed to provide direct evidence of this. The '*hypothese functionelle*' (functional hypothesis) suggests that the bilateral dis-

charges lead to a functional exclusion of the language centres in which even
the possible remedial function of the minor hemisphere is cut off by the
abnormal discharges. Dulac, Billard and Arthius (1983) concluded that the
aphasia was the result of 'functional disorganisation of the language centres
due to important intercortical EEG abnormalities', which they described as
being similar to Todd's paralysis of language. Worster-Drought (1971)
considered it probable that the pathological agent was a slow-working
encephalitic virus and reported that a similar condition, commonly known
as 'hard pad', occurred in dogs. The debate regarding the pathology of the
condition remains unresolved.

The syndrome was first described by Landau and Kleffner in 1957. Six
children aged 5-9 years at onset, who presented with receptive aphasia in
association with a range of convulsive behaviours, were discussed.
However, as Lees and Neville (1990) pointed out, a range of pathological
mechanisms was implicated in the original paper. Of the five children
described, the first had several periods of seizures, which were associated
with a positive motor phenomenon on the right side, and evidence of a
family history of various seizure disorders. The second case was, in fact, a
sibling of the first. This child's history included two minor head injuries in
short succession. Although there had been few studies of the effects of
minor head trauma on a child's development, minor head injury was also
mentioned in the fourth case. Generalised convulsions were a late sequela
in the second child. Grand mal seizures occurred in the third case, as well as
localised seizures of the left face. The fifth child's language regression began
about 1 month after mumps. A later sequela was a grand mal seizure. Three
of the children had a history of more than one period of aphasia and their
condition appeared to have a fluctuating course. This summary demonstrates some of the difficulties of separating the Landau–Kleffner syndrome
from the more general convulsive aphasias. This later group will be discussed in Chapter 6.

There is still considerable debate about what does and what does not
constitute a case of the Landau-Kleffner syndrome. For Lees and Neville
(1990), the neuropathology of this group was due to 'an organic event
occurring with epilepsy' which did not fulfil the other criteria for convulsive aphasias. Clearly, this definition by exclusion requires further work but
I believe that it is important to try to distinguish between the Landau–
Kleffner syndrome and other convulsive aphasias. Neuropathology has
implications for natural history, management and prognosis. However, in
the summary of previous studies presented in this book, I accept that in
some series there is a mix of the two groups; some clinicians call all
convulsive aphasias the Landau-Kleffner syndrome and others make some
distinction on the basis of presumed pathology.

The exact relationship between the aphasia and the convulsive disorder
in the Landau–Kleffner syndrome has not been established. The suggestion,

by Dulac, Billard and Arthuis (1983), that paroxysmal discharges act in some way to block access to the language areas of the cortex bears some relation to the phenomenon of aphasic arrest, which was described by Penfield and Rasmussen (1950) in their studies of adults undergoing electrical stimulation of the cortex during neurosurgery for intractable epilepsy. This view has recently been reinforced by the adoption of surgical techniques to manage severe cases of the Landau–Kleffner syndrome (Morrell, Whistler and Black, 1989; Smith, Whistler and Morrell, 1989); this will be discussed later.

Bishop (1985) reviewed 45 cases from the literature (followed up to 12 years of age) to discuss the variable of age of onset in relation to outcome. She agreed with the widely held clinical view that the older the child at onset the better the prognosis. This is the opposite to the situation in children having aphasia from unilateral cerebral lesions, in whom prognosis for recovery is poorer with increasing age. Although the Landau–Kleffner syndrome is not a common condition, the number of new cases published since 1978 has increased significantly (Beaumanoir, 1985). However, Beaumanoir's statement that 'familial and personal medical history are irrelevant and there are no associated neurological signs' is not upheld by a careful analysis of either the original series (Landau and Kleffner, 1957) or subsequent reports. Only further systematic study will determine this.

Natural history of the Landau–Kleffner syndrome

The literature contains single case studies, small group studies and retrospective analysis of previously reported cases. There is little general agreement about the course and prognosis of the syndrome. Landau and Kleffner (1957) themselves optimistically declared that the prognosis for their children was good, although few objective data were available for their group. More recent studies have attempted to provide this information, although most series, particularly with long-term follow-up, are small.

Worster-Drought (1971) described 14 children: 9 showed considerable improvement and in 5 a severe degree of receptive aphasia persisted after many years. It was an inability to describe a clinically uniform picture for Landau–Kleffner syndrome, both in reviewing cases in the literature and in six of their own cases, that led Deonna et al. (1977) to postulate that it was a heterogeneous syndrome, with at least three courses. The first group, with the better prognosis, had a rapid onset and a rapid recovery of the aphasia. The second group showed progressive worsening of the aphasia after repeated seizures, and there were subsequent aphasic episodes. The third group also showed a progressive receptive aphasia, but there were no clinical seizures and recovery was variable. This study was not the first to mention fluctuating aphasic episodes (Landau and Kleffner's original paper also does), but they were the first to see this group as presenting a slightly different course and prognosis. Only further research will determine whether these three subgroups do exist, have the same underlying pathology and therefore really are variations on the Landau–Kleffner syndrome.

The length of time that reported cases of this syndrome have been followed up varies considerably among studies. This is an important consideration in terms of our understanding of the natural history of the condition. Van Harskamp, Van Dongen and Loonen (1978), in describing a case that they followed up for 7 years post-onset, stated that, although the seizures had been medically controlled and EEG abnormalities improved, there had not been a parallel improvement in the child's aphasia. This girl was followed up annually until 18 years of age; at that age Van Dongen et al. (1989) reported that subtle language deficits were still apparent and her EEG still showed mild abnormalities.

Mantovani and Landau (1980), in following up the six cases originally described by Landau and Kleffner and three new cases, found that in five of them there was a good recovery to essentially normal language by adulthood. Their statement 'the variability in outcome of similarly affected children remains one of the most puzzling features of this disorder' is echoed by most researchers in their attempts to find common denominators, and frequently they review as many of the previously reported cases in an attempt to do just this. As discussed earlier, Bishop (1985) showed a relationship between age at onset and prognosis.

Ripley and Lea (1984) attempted to provide such data in their follow-up study of ex-pupils of a school for children with speech and language disorders who had severe receptive language problems. Of the 14 children discussed 10 would appear, from case histories supplied, to have an acquired basis for their disorder. Neuropathology was as potentially varied as the Landau and Kleffner (1957) series and included evidence of mild head trauma, epilepsy and cerebral infection. Information about socio-economic status of the 10, and achievements since leaving school, shows that two were married and all were in full-time paid employment. Only two of the ex-pupils had ongoing health problems; one had migraine and another had epilepsy. At best they all had limited verbal communication, and most continued to rely on sign language to communicate.

The variable clinical picture has led to some debate about the core features of the condition, the typical course and the most effective management. It has been suggested that such a wide range of possibilities is hardly likely to represent one syndrome. Moreover, because the condition has rarely been comprehensively described from the language point of view, equally wide ranging reports about the possible presenting language symptoms exist.

There would appear to be increasing recognition that only multicentre longitudinal studies will help to further our understanding of the course and prognosis of the Landau-Kleffner syndrome. Dugas et al. (1991) pointed out that most studies have approached the subject from one of three different objectives: to describe the condition and its various patterns and allow them to be distinguished; to consider the influence of the various variables such as age of onset with regard to the pathology and nature of the primary disorder; and to consider the early effects of rehabilitation and pharmacological therapies (therapeutic objectives). For further discussion of the natural history, course and prognosis of the Landau-Kleffner syndrome, they selected 33 cases from 156 cases published between 1957 and 1989. These cases were selected based on the following criteria:

1. Regression of language after a period of normal development.
2. Existence of epileptic seizures and/or paroxysmal EEG abnormalities.
3. Sufficient information for a multidimensional approach to prognosis.
4. Follow-up to the minimum age of 14 years.

The age of onset of these cases varied from 2 to 10 years with most being between 4 and 6 years. Dugas et al. defined four outcome groups:

1. Very unfavourable outcome (four cases), in which there was no social or professional independence, almost total comprehension deficit and no oral expression.
2. Unfavourable outcome (11 cases), in which there was some degree of socioprofessional skill, and a severe communication disability, in which oral language was unintelligible or significantly reduced.
3. Favourable outcome (11 cases), in which they gained good socioprofessional skills and where the persistence of oral and/or written language difficulties did not impede communication.
4. Very favourable outcome (seven cases) in which they all lived independently without difficulty and there was no observable communication difficulty, oral or written.

Dugas et al. presented a detailed account of the symptoms of language disturbances seen in these groups and concluded by asking 'whether the length of the follow-up influences the rating of the prognosis'.

After several years of seeing children with this syndrome in clinical practice, some data have been produced from a small but highly variable group of children (some of these are reported in Lees, 1989). The children have ranged in age at onset from 2 to 12 years. Some have presented acutely and in others there has been a period of language deterioration lasting over several weeks to several months. Those with the longer period of deterioration seem to have poorer prognosis. Complete verbal auditory agnosia has been seen in a number of cases, although this is not always the major symptom, and the receptive language component may fluctuate. In others verbal language is absent or considerably reduced. Older children may present with a rather pedantic conversational style with inappropriate prosody. Data from Lees (1989) suggest that children who do not make progress to within − 2 standard deviations in verbal comprehension within 6 months of onset are in the poor outcome group. Most of these children required special educational provision within a specialised teaching environment; in this visual methods of teaching language (signing and reading) were backed up with an emphasis on functional communication for everyday life.

Role of the speech and language therapist

The characteristic language problem of children with the Landau–Kleffner syndrome is a severe receptive aphasia. This has been variously described. Cooper and Ferry (1978) preferred to call it a verbal auditory agnosia rather than an aphasia. This suggests a view that in these children, this syndrome is not a primary language disorder but rather an auditory processing disorder. Indeed many of the children are initially thought to be deaf, but on examination peripheral hearing is normal. In order to investigate whether the comprehension problems of children with the Landau–Kleffner syndrome were restricted to the auditory modality, Bishop (1982) set up a study using three forms of a test for the comprehension of grammatical structures (later called the Test for Reception of Grammar, TROG, Bishop, 1983). Three groups of children, one with Landau–Kleffner syndrome, one with developmental language disorder of an expressive type, and normal controls were tested with spoken, written and signed presentations of the test. Results confirmed that the children with the Landau–Kleffner syndrome had deviant comprehension of language, in auditory, signed and written presentation. However, a subsequent experiment with deaf children demonstrated that they had a very similar profile of difficulty in comprehension of language to that of the children with Landau–Kleffner syndrome. Bishop suggests that this similarity is the result of an auditory processing difficulty in the Landau–Kleffner syndrome which then forces the children to rely on the visual modality to learn the grammar of the language, as deaf children do.

Reported language problems are not confined to receptive language. Case histories can reveal pre-existing difficulties in language acquisition as in one child in the study of Ripley and Lea (1984). Dugas et al. (1976) reported word-finding difficulty, perseveration, phonemic and semantic paraphasias in the verbal language of the 9-year-old girl they describe; these were also observed to a lesser degree in her written language. Not so many papers concentrate on the expressive language problems in the Landau–Kleffner syndrome, and none has tried to explain their occurrence, although it seems less likely that they could be accounted for by the 'auditory deprivation' model suggested by Bishop (1982) for the receptive problems.

Van der Sandt-Koenderman et al. (1984) also reported a child who produced paraphasias and neologisms. They found that the frequency of these in spontaneous speech was a very sensitive indicator of language breakdown and recovery. Beaumanoir (1985) supported the view that when the onset of aphasia occurs after the child has acquired written language, and if this knowledge is retained, then there is a better prognosis for educational attainment.

As yet, few studies have presented details about speech and language therapy and educational rehabilitation of children with the Landau–Kleffner syndrome. One exception is the detailed case study, by Vance (1991), of a child who presented with slow deterioration in language starting at 3;6 years, and which lasted for over 8 months. This child was first introduced to signing through the Makaton Vocabulary (Walker, 1980) and later through the Paget–Gorman Sign System (Paget, Gorman and Paget, 1976), producing strings of seven or more signs by the age of 7 years. Other specific therapeutic methods used included the introduction of Cued Articulation (Passy, 1990), a series of hand shapes that identify each English consonant. These methods were used in individual therapy and in the classroom, where other educational techniques included a daily picture diary to help develop the concept of time and a colour pattern scheme for literacy skills (Lea, 1965, 1979). Other communication skills taught included auditory training and interaction skills. This boy went on to attend a unit for the partially hearing where signing was used. The approach, outlined by Vance, is still undergoing development at the unit she described.

In their discussion of speech and language therapy for the Landau–Kleffner syndrome, Gerard, Dugas and Sagar (1991) stated: 'choice between alternative systems and a reconstruction of oral language seems ... an oversimplified approach to the discussion.' They reviewed the management of 18 children of whom 5 received no speech and language therapy. As a result of the difficulty in obtaining details of the treatment given in the other cases, most of their information is rather general. Of nine children who received therapy the following methods were reported as being used at some stage: auditory therapy, phonemic analysis, modelling verbal expression, written language, symbols and signs. However, whereas Vance (1991) was able to give some indication of how specific methods were introduced for her one case, Gerard, Dugas and Sagar (1991) were only able to give some indication of the duration of speech therapy in 13 cases; the therapy lasted for between 3 months and 10 years. However, one case was reported in detail and Gerard et al. propose a therapeutic model based on a neuro-psychological approach. They concluded that, when the limitations of speech and language therapy were taken into account, therapy should always aim to build on the residual language abilities of children with the

Landau-Kleffner syndrome, and expanded on this: 'when these are too insufficient, or when the intellectual potential does not allow one to be compelled to systematic, associative learning, creating a potential for lexical representation, then no more can be expected of sign language.' In such cases they advocated the use of 'minimal systems of communication using gesture, iconic or pictographic symbols', preferring the latter for their flexibility.

De Wijngaert (1991) also recognised that there was little information in the literature concerning language therapy or educational methods. His preferred approach to these children is one in which speech and language therapy is integrated into the classroom programme to provide a comprehensive programme for educational needs. It is essentially an oral programme and is based on 9 years of work with six children having the Landau-Kleffner syndrome. The programme is based on creating the right environment for learning for these children; for de Wijngaert this means creating enthusiasm. He provided some indications of the ways in which oral and written language skills are taught and advocated that this should be done in stages. The Colour Pattern Scheme (Lea, 1965, 1979) was also used with these children. Unfortunately, no specific details about how children progressed with this programme were provided.

This summary should serve to emphasise the amount of work still to be done on speech and language rehabilitation of children with the Landau-Kleffner syndrome. Unlike Landau (1991), I cannot agree that the use of single case studies represents what he called 'a stupid level of speculation'. Also I would not advocate the use of randomised control trials as he did. I do believe that small numbers make multicentre collaboration essential, but like Vance (1991), Gerard, Dugas and Sagar (1991) and de Wijngaert (1991), I also believe that carefully constructed programmes in which therapy and education work together, probably along a neuropsychological model, would be a sensible place to start to provide some of the details which are now required.

Other aspects of the management of the Landau–Kleffner syndrome

It is obvious from the literature reviewed so far that the complex nature of this syndrome has meant that it has attracted interest from a wide range of professionals. In clinical practice the proper management of children with the Landau-Kleffner syndrome requires a multidisciplinary team. As a result of the nature of the condition, this may mean liaison among many centres; certainly, this will require multi-professional working between health and educational services. This kind of working can be difficult and communication among the various professionals, and also between professionals and the family, can break down. If this is to be avoided it can be helpful to appoint a key worker for each child responsible for coordinating relay of information among the professionals and also to the family. The professional chosen to be the key worker will depend on the child's situation; it may be necessary to change the key worker if educational placement changes or if the family moves. Although it has been traditional for those in the medical professions to head teams along rather hierarchical lines, there is some evidence to suggest that this may slowly be changing. A team of professional equals in which one member is chosen as key worker according to the child's needs at that time is preferred. Where the child is in special education this could be a teacher or educational psychologist, whereas in the preschool period a therapist or health visitor could be more appropriate. The family should, where possible, be fully involved in the choice of key worker, and the development of a good relationship between family and key worker should be a matter of priority.

Alongside the speech and language therapist and educational staff, those involved in the management of children with the Landau-Kleffner syndrome will probably include the audiologist and the paediatric neurologist. In the early stages of diagnosis, it is important to establish the child's audiological status. Children with this syndrome are often initially thought to be hearing impaired. The high incidence of conductive hearing loss in childhood, most commonly secondary to otitis media, means that it is important to rule out this cause of deterioration in language skills. Equally, even after a diagnosis of the Landau-Kleffner syndrome is made, a child's hearing will require regular monitoring to ensure that it remains as stable as possible, and that any treatable conditions are dealt with promptly because fluctuating hearing added to the language problem can lead to further problems with both communication and behaviour.

Two other aspects of the management of the Landau-Kleffner syndrome warrant careful review: the use of anticonvulsant medication and, more recently, surgical intervention. A number of papers have reported the successful use of a range of anticonvulsants with small numbers of children with this syndrome. McKinney and McGreal (1974) reported good results using steroids with six patients. Dugas et al. (1976) used phenobarbitone (phenobarbital) in one case and claimed 'spectacular regression of the aphasia' although no formal measures of language function were given.

Five children were reported by Marescaux et al. (1990), who also reviewed some previous reports. They stated that 'phenobarbital, carbamazepine and phenytoin were ineffective or worsened the EEG and neuropsychological symptoms, whereas valproate, ethosuximide and benzodiazepines were partially or transiently efficacious'. Dextroamphetamine was said to produce a dramatic but transient improvement in EEG abnormalities in one of two children, but had no effect on language disturbance. By contrast corticosteroid treatment resulted in both improvement of speech and normalisation of EEGs in three children. Marescaux et al. therefore concluded, from their own experience and from the literature, that 'corticosteroids should be given in high doses as soon as the diagnosis is firmly established and should be continued ... for several months or years'. Although EEGs are included in the paper, formal language test scores are not reported. It should be noted that the cases described in this chapter have been treated with a wide range of anticonvulsants and that variable effects are reported. Careful monitoring of language when anticonvulsants are being used is recommended.

Multiple subpial transection was described by Morrell, Whistler and Beck (1989) as 'a new approach to the surgical treatment of focal epilepsy'. They recommended its use in those patients whose epileptogenic lesions lie in the regions of the cerebral cortex that control speech, movement, primary sensation or memory. The procedure selectively severs certain horizontal intercortical neural fibres but preserves vertical ones with the aim of reducing 'the likelihood of occurrence of synchronized cell discharge and to do so in a manner which does not impair the major functional capacity of the tissue'. They reported ten patients in whom this procedure had been carried out directly to Broca's or Wernicke's areas, all of whom continued to be verbal language users post-surgery. In the evaluation of recovery by Morrell et al., no formal measures of language function were reported. There is a move to start using this technique with a small number of children with the Landau–Kleffner syndrome, although its effects have not been documented in detail.

Examples of children with the Landau–Kleffner syndrome

Case 12: a child with acute onset, rapid recovery and good prognosis

This boy (first described in Lees and Neville, 1990) had a history of normal developmental when he presented with an acute aphasia at age 12;6 years. He reported a feeling of discomfort in his right arm which he described as 'like an electric shock'. EEG revealed bilateral temporal spikes and the sensations suggest a persisting dysrhythmic element. CT scan was normal. The lack of other pathological evidence lead to a diagnosis of the Landau–Kleffner syndrome. Initially, he presented with a severe receptive and expressive aphasia. This gradually resolved but not without some fluctuations in verbal comprehension. Pure-tone audiometry con-firmed normal hearing. Expressive language contained both jargon and paraphasias. He received no further speech and language

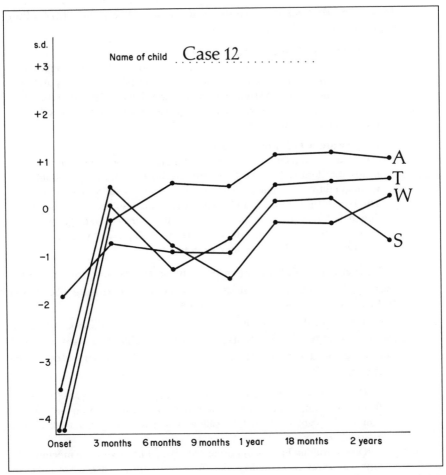

Figure 5.1 Profile of recovery of Case 12: A, auditory association; S, sentence repetition; T, TROG; W, Word Finding Vocabulary Test

therapy after his discharge from hospital. Apart from the reported mild fluctuations in verbal comprehension, the course of recovery from aphasia was unremarkable. There were no seizures. Within the 2 years of follow-up his language test scores returned to the normal range. He continued to make reasonable progress with his peers in a mainstream comprehensive school. Figure 5.1 records his progress on language assessments during the 2 years of follow-up.

Results from the story-telling test at onset revealed a jargon aphasia characterised by inappropriate unfinished sentences:

Dog Story (initial assessment):
'Is it the middle bit? He the thing in. The thing was up really.'

However, this resolved quite quickly as subsequent story-telling examples demonstrate:

Farmer Story (3 months post-onset):
'A old farmer had a lazy donkey. The farmer wanted to put the donkey in the barn. He pushed him, then he pulled him but the donkey didn't move. So he asked the lazy dog to bark at the donkey. The dog refused. So the co-operative cat scratched the dog. The dog began to bark and the donkey jumped into the barn.'

Farmer Story (12 months post-onset):
'There was an old farmer who had a stubborn donkey. The farmer wants to get the donkey into the barn. First he pushed him but the donkey wouldn't move. Then he pulled him but the donkey still wouldn't move. The farmer thought he could frighten the donkey so he tried to get the dog to bark . . . to frighten the donkey. But it . . . refused. So he got the cat to scratch the dog to make the dog bark. That, that didn't work er . . . er . . . The dog barked. The donkey went in.'

He made a small number of paraphasic errors on confrontational naming tests, all of which gradually decreased during the 2-year follow-up period as shown in Table 5.1.

Written language was never severely affected as this example of spontaneous writing soon after onset of the disorder shows: [spelling and punctuation as original, brackets mark self-corrected errors in the original]

'One Harvest Monday I was combining my feild when I came across this mole, I didn't want to run him down so I picked him up and took him in the cab. I decided to call him a name "Fred". I took him everywhere I went.

'One morning I had a [fo] phone call saying I had to go to a meeting a long way a way, so I couldn't take "fred" with me. So I asked a freind to look after him for me. The freind was a busy person too who just this once he thought he would let him loose in the garden. 5 minutes later the friend looked around and saw the mole was squashed on the road.'

Table 5.1   Paraphasic errors on tests of confrontational naming for Case 12

Date from onset	Item	Response	Error type
Onset	Sling	Slung	Phonemic paraphasia
	Crutch	Clutch	Phonemic paraphasia
	Watering can	Bucket	Semantic paraphasia
	Lighthouse	Lightbulb	Semantic paraphasia
6 months	Corkscrew	Screwdriver	Semantic paraphasia
9 months	Sporran	Spirren	Phonemic paraphasia
18 months	Handcuffs	Cufflinks	Semantic paraphasia

Case 13: a child with repeated seizures and gradual worsening of the aphasia, with subsequent aphasic periods and good recovery

This boy had a history of early feeding difficulties and delay in speech and motor development. He was said by his parents to be slightly slower than his older sister, but this did not give cause for more specific concern. At the age of 4;9 years he was reported to have had a left-sided focal attack progressing to grand mal, with transient left-sided weakness afterwards, He was treated with phenytoin. There was a further episode at the age of 7 years: shaking in the left arm spreading to the left leg and lasting for approximately 20 minutes, followed by transient left-sided weakness. An EEG at the age of 7;6 years showed a right mid-temporal and frontoparietal focus. At the age of 9 years there was a deterioration in his school performance: noticeable pausing in his speech, dropping things from the left hand and some episodes of eye blinking. The phenytoin was increased. An IQ assessment at this time showed a low average intelligence and there was some gradual improvement recorded when he was re-tested a year later. At this time some mild ataxia of his left arm was noticed, and he was having episodes of dribbling, jerking and apparent deafness. He was treated with sodium valproate. At the age of 10 years it was clear that he did not understand what was said to him and he was admitted for investigations. Treatment with a ketogenic diet produced a possibly transient improvement. Corticosteroids were ineffective. He continued to be treated with phenytoin to the age of 14 years. It was observed, both at school and at home, that phenytoin in the upper end of the therapeutic range had some significant effect on his comprehension, and informal clinical observation confirmed that there was some evidence of this.

A CT scan at 11 years of age was normal, as were brain-stem evoked auditory responses. An EEG performed around the same time showed a background rhythm that was rather slower than the previous record. The left temporal abnormality was much more marked. There were sharp waves in the rolandic areas, predominantly on the right side. In addition there was a focal sharp and slow wave abnormality in the left temporoparietal region suggesting a focal abnormality. It had been quite difficult to maintain the correct phenytoin dose in the top end of the range, and there were signs associated with mild phenytoin toxicity from time to time. There was no persisting physical deficit and his overt fits were fully controlled by the age of 11 years.

He was admitted to a school for speech- and language-disordered children at the age of 12 years. His Performance IQ on the WISC was 92. His hearing was confirmed as within the normal range for speech. He made good progress in language although high level auditory–verbal processing problems did persist. At 13;7 years his Schonell Spelling score was at an age equivalent of 11;6 years. At the same time his Neale Reading score was at an age equivalent of 11;9 years for accuracy and 11;2 years for comprehension. He was transferred back to a mainstream comprehensive school at 14 years where he passed four GCSE's. He went on, at 17 years, to attend further education to train in furniture and cabinet making. At 19 he completed his course and won a 5-year apprenticeship with a furniture-making company.

It is often difficult to establish the pre-aphasic language abilities of children with ACA. An example of this boy's expressive language was taped by his family when he was 6 years old [family audio and video tapes can provide a useful source for information about previous language abilities]:

'One day the old man planted a seed...a turnip seed and...um the old man....one day...he said "Grow strong, grow strong, grow, grow". So the turnip did grow strong and grow...and ..the um...one day when he came out to pick it the old m.. man.. he pulled and he pulled but he couldn't get it up.

'He got the old woman. The old woman pulled the man. The man pulled the turnip, but it still wouldn't come up. So the old lady got the granddaughter and the granddaughter pulled the .... uh .. the old lady. The lady began to pull the old man. The old man began to pull the turnip but it still wouldn't come up. So the um....grandaughter got the dog. The dog pulled the granddaughter. The granddaughter pulled the ... old lady. The old lady pulled the old man. The old man pulled the turnip but it still wouldn't come up. So the dog collected the cat and the cat pulled the dog and the dog pulled the granddaughter. The granddaughter pulled the old lady. The old lady pulled the man and .... and the old lady pulled the man and the man pulled the turnip...but it still wouldn't come up. So old man.. um... um... um pulled the turnip but he still couldn't get it up.

This example of pre-aphasic written language was taken from school work at age 9 years:

'If I drove the London bus it would be very bumpy and uncomfortable, and when it rains the people who sit at the top will get quite wet. When it's sunny the people downstairs would get hot. To start the bus you have to wind up a handle and the bus is washed every week. So it is in good condition. If someone leaned over the top of the bus it might be dangerous. I would like to have a bus of my own.'

These examples of story telling were recorded during follow-up, 2;2 years and 3;9 years post-onset respectively:

Farmer Story (2;2 years post-onset):
'There was a very stubborn and very lazy donkey. The farmer wanted him to go in the barn. He pushed him and he didn't move. He pulled him too. The farmer had a good idea to frighten the donkey. He asked the dog to bark at the donkey but he refused not to. So he asked the cat to scratch him. The cat scratched the dog. The dog began to bark loudly. The barking frightened the donkey and he went in the barn.'

Farmer Story (3;9 years post-onset):
'There was an old farmer who wanted to put his donkey in the barn. But the donkey would not move because he was stubborn. First he pushed him, then he pulled him but he still wouldn't move. So he asked the dog to bark at him but the lazy dog refused. So he asked the cooperative cat to scratch the dog to get the dog to bark. The cat scratched the dog and the dog barked and the donkey went in the barn.'

Figure 5.2 shows the profile of his recovery.

Case 14: a child with progressively deteriorating language, no seizures and little recovery

This boy's developmental history was described as normal, although there was some language delay with first words at 18 months and with phrases at 4 years. This was first diagnosed by a speech and language therapist who saw him at the age of 4 years. He had speech and language therapy for 1 year. Six months after starting speech and language therapy, a conductive bilateral hearing loss of 30–40 dB was diagnosed. Myringotomies and adenoid-ectomy were performed a year later. At that time his speech began to deteriorate and this was confirmed by the local speech and language therapist. At the age of 5;7 years his score on the Reynell Developmental Language Scales (RDLS) for verbal comprehension was below the 2-year level. However, he was started in a main-stream school and his teacher suspected that he had a hearing problem. By the age of 9 years his verbal comprehension was nil except for some slight situational understanding. An EEG per-formed at the age of 6 years showed an epileptic pattern but there were no overt fits. His IQ, measured on the Leiter International Scale at the same age, was recorded as 80. At the age of 7;3 years it was measured again as 75.

At the age of 9 years his motor function and dexterity were assessed as being below the 5-year level and he was described as markedly dyspraxic. His was left handed. His hearing was at 40 dB

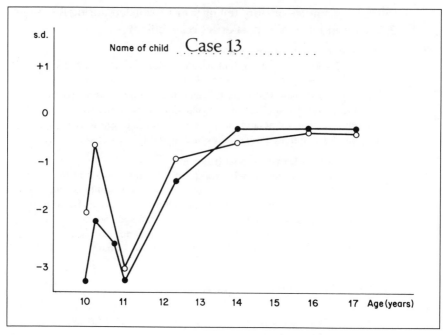

Figure 5.2   Profile of recovery of Case 13: (●) receptive language; (○) expressive language

for most frequencies, and at 65–70 dB for 250 Hz. Another EEG was taken at the age of 10;4 years and was also described as 'markedly epileptic'. He never had an overt fit, although there were one or two suspicious episodes. He had been receiving phenytoin as an anticonvulsant since age 6 years. This was gradually and success-fully withdrawn from the age of 13 years. His acquired receptive aphasia was described as one preceded by a period of near-normal language development and followed by a fade-out of receptive skills. He finished his education at a school for the deaf because he relied entirely on signed language for communication.

Language assessment scores

- Onset of aphasia at age 6;6 years
- Three months post-onset, RDLS verbal comprehension was below the 2-year level
- Three and a half years later, RDLS verbal comprehension was nil, but using Paget–Gorman Signs a 3-year level was recorded.

Assessed at the age of 14 years his score on the Test for Reception of Grammar was 2, a z-score of -10. When the same test was presented so that he could read the sentences, his score improved to 16.

Case 15: a child with progressively deteriorating language, later development of seizures and variable recovery

This girl (first described by Lees and Urwin, 1991) presented at the age of 6;9 years with a history of a slow deterioration in language skills that had started 9 months previously. Before this she had been developing normally and had attended a mainstream infant school. There was no family history of speech and language problems. She had no history of epilepsy. Initially, the problem had been perceived as a fluctuating hearing loss but all audiological investigations were normal. By the time she was referred for this assessment, she only understood simple phrases in situational context. Her expressive language was reduced to simple stereotyped phrases. Her behaviour was difficult to manage at school. Neurological examination was normal throughout, as was a CT scan. EEG revealed a focus of abnormal activity in the left temporal lobe. There were no overt fits. She did complain of not sleeping well and of a pain in her left ear, but no explanation could be found for this. Her IQ on the WISC(R) was Full-scale 71, Performance 91 and Verbal 55. She passed two blocks on the TROG, understanding single nouns and single verbs only. She produced a number of errors on the Word Finding Vocabulary Test (WFVT), including irrelevant stereotypes or requests for her mother to respond on her behalf. The changes in these test scores over 2 ½ years are shown in Figure 5.3. For a trial period, she received carbamazepine to see if verbal comprehension would improve. It was unchanged 6 weeks later. Corticosteroids were introduced instead, for a trial period, and discontinued 6 weeks later when verbal comprehension still remained unchanged. Her behaviour deteriorated further. After this, all anticonvulsants were withdrawn with no further effect.

Observations of her at school and home indicated that she understood very little. Her deteriorating behaviour was directly related to her lack of comprehension. She was reluctant to be parted from her mother and relied heavily on her for 'translation' of what was happening or being said. She would turn her mother's face towards her when she wanted such an explanation and also used the same technique if she was trying to tell her mother something (behaviour that is fairly common in young language-disordered children with severe comprehension problems). A statement of educational need was drawn up and she was placed in a language unit at the age of 7;4 years.

A system of language teaching through reading, based on the Colour Pattern Scheme (Lea, 1970), was used to work on comprehension of language through visual media. She was also taught

Table 5.2   Expressive language and naming for Case 15

From the Action Picture Test at age 9;3 years:
1. A girl sitting ... cuddle (+ Makaton sign for teddy).
2. The girl... the mum .. . put shoe in.
3. The dog ... the man stay in... the dog stuck.
4. The horse... jumping under.
5. The cat ... eating the mouse.
6. The girl up ... the girl down ... running on the floor ... she brok her eyes (+ gesture for glasses).
7. The mum ... a girl is boy up (+ gesture for stamp) is in.
8. The man ... going up the house... the man... trying to get the cat.
9. The boy .... the boy... the shoe ... the dog eat and the boy crying.
10. The mum ... and the bag... ball.. a lot... and the boy drop it on the floor.

From the Word Finding Vocabulary Test at age 9;3 years:

Item	Response	Comment
Cup	Cup	+ Makaton sign
Table	Table	+ Makaton sign
Boat	Boat	+ Makaton sign
Tree	Tree	+ Makaton sign
Key	Like a door key	+ Makaton sign
Knife	Dinner	Semantic paraphasia
Window	Glass	Semantic paraphasia
Finger	Hand	Semantic paraphasia
Duck	Bird	Semantic paraphasia
Snake	Snake	
Basket	Bag	Semantic paraphasia + gesture
Saw	Cut	
Pear	*Unintelligible*	Neologism
Clown	Queen	Semantic paraphasia
Case	Bag... go work	
Bear	Bag... bear	Self-corrected
Moon	In the dark... when you sleep	
Chimney	House	Semantic paraphasia
Kangaroo	/kærə/	Neologism
Kite	/kærə/ you hold up	Perseverated neologism
Camel	/kærə/ sometimes two	Perseverated neologism
Squirrel	Squirrel	
Leaf	A tree one	
Owl	Dark ... a bird dark	
Snail		Gesture

the Makaton Vocabulary (Walker, 1980) but was reluctant to use more than a few single signs. Listening and attention work were also encouraged as was basic sentence construction work. Her expressive language was essentially non-fluent and telegrammatic with both phonemic and semantic paraphasias and neologisms, as well as perseverations (Table 5.2). With no change in her verbal comprehension it was clear that she was likely to require long-term placement in a school for children with speech and language disorders. At the age of 9;3 years, 2½ years post-onset, she was referred for a neurosurgical assessment to see if she would be a suitable candidate for multiple subpial transection; a decision on this is still awaited.

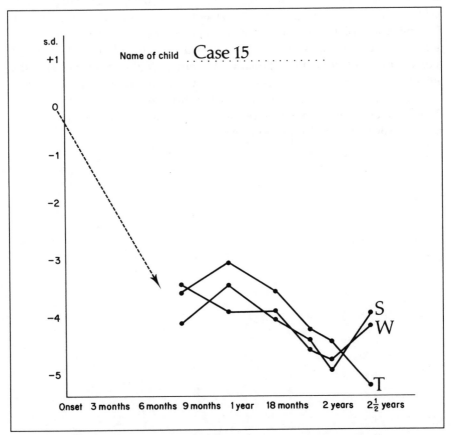

Figure 5.3 Profile of recovery of Case 15: A, auditory association; S, sentence repetition; T, TROG; W, Word Finding Vocabulary Test. (Dotted line marks presumed course of deterioration)

Conclusions about children with the Landau–Kleffner syndrome.

Some of the variablity of the Landau–Kleffner syndrome has been presented here, including cases of acute and prolonged onset, as well as those with variable and fluctuating course, good and poor recovery. Some of the dilemmas associated with diagnosis and management of the syndrome have also been outlined, including recent studies of the use of anticonvulsants and neurosurgery in management. Overall it is clear that more long-term detailed studies of the Landau–Kleffner syndrome are required to improve our understanding of the management of these children.

The evidence suggests that a number of variables interact to influence the course and prognosis of the disorder. Indeed, we may go on to discover that the Landau–Kleffner syndrome is really a number of related conditions with different neuropathologies. Meanwhile, continued confusion about this disorder points to the need for multicentre studies using an agreed protocol for both short-term monitoring of management with anticonvulsants and determination of the outcome of surgery, as well as clearly presented detailed case studies of long-term follow-up of the effects of language remediation and education. Equally, the rarity of the disorders and the distressing effect that its relentless course can have on both child and family, points to the need for support for those with this condition. This should include the cooperation of the voluntary sector where appropriate as the burden of care can be very heavy.

Chapter 6
Other convulsive aphasias

Pathology and natural history

For those unfamiliar with convulsive aphasias then this chapter may introduce a number of previously unconsidered ideas. It is reasonable to ask what is the underlying cause of the seizure activity with which a child presents. This chapter was written because of a previous failure to identify and substantiate the possible mechanisms underlying convulsive aphasia in the literature.

The division of the convulsive group of aphasias into the Landau-Kleffner syndrome and other convulsive aphasias poses a number of problems. Although the neuropathological mechanism underlying the Landau-Kleffner syndrome has not been fully identified, its place as a subdivision of the convulsive aphasias is supported by the belief that, whatever the mechanism, it is related to convulsive activity. Previous reports in the literature of convulsive aphasias in childhood have complicated the problem further because in many the descriptions make it difficult to separate possible cases of Landau-Kleffner syndrome from other convulsive aphasias. Indeed, in the original paper by Landau and Kleffner (1957) in which the syndrome was first described, it is possible, from the descriptions, to identify a whole host of different possible mechanisms, including minor head trauma and convulsive status. It is certainly possible that some of reports of Landau-Kleffner syndrome in the literature are in fact other types of convulsive aphasia and some of the reports of convulsive aphasia might be called Landau-Kleffner syndrome by other writers. Some researchers dismiss this problem, including Dugas et al. (1991) who said that 'authors who have been involved with the question of the evolution of LK syndrome have generally been cautious in using restrictive criteria of inclusion'.

The reason for this confusion is, in part, a result of failure to take a detailed look at the possible mechanisms that can be identified as underlying convulsive aphasias. Lees and Neville (1990) proposed a classification of convulsive aphasias which identified a number of potential mechanisms. They said:

> The convulsive group could include children who lose language comprehension by a number of different mechanisms:
> 1. As a consequence of convulsive status.
> 2. As a post-ictal phenomenon (Todd's paresis).
> 3. As a consequence of the primary pathology, e.g. temporal lobe inflammatory or malignant disease.
> 4. As a feature of minor epileptic status.
> 5. As a psychological reaction to epilepsy
> 6. As an organic event occurring with epilepsy but not fullfilling the criteria 1-5.

Of course categories 1, 2, 4, 5 and 6 required further definition because the original cause of the seizure disorder could need further investigation. However, for Lees and Neville (1990), the Landau–Kleffner syndrome was the sixth category and these children have already been described in Chapter 5. This chapter is concerned with the first five of the proposed groups, recognising that we are still some way from understanding the sixth group in depth. As far as I am aware no previous studies of convulsive aphasia have discussed these possible mechanisms and this provisional categorisation.

The phenomenon of aphasic arrest caused by electrical stimulation of the cerebral cortex was described by Penfield and Rassmussen (1950) in their neurosurgical work on intractable epilepsy. Figure 6.1 shows a diagram of the cerebral cortex according to this model. More recent work has identified other aspects of aphasic arrest including the interference with comprehension by the electrical stimulation of Wernicke's area (Lesser et al., 1986). These observations make it clear that language comprehension and production can be affected by artificial electrical stimulation, and provide the basis of the hypothesis that abnormal electrical discharges of the cerebral cortex, which occur in convulsive disorder, can produce aphasias.

Epilepsy is known to coexist with, or develop as a sequela of, a range of childhood conditions in which there is CNS involvement. Corbett (1985) gives figures for incidence of involvement ranging from 6% (in children with IQ of 50–70) to almost 50% (in those of IQ < 20). For children with specific language difficulties, Robinson (1987, 1991) reported 21% with a definite history of seizures and a further 11% where the history was 'questionable' regarding seizures. In the 1991 paper he stated that this was 'an unexpectedly high frequency of previous seizures' when compared with the 5-7% in the general population, and proposed three hypotheses to account for this: first, that 'the seizures themselves might cause the language disorder by interfering with brain function'; against this hypothesis he said that the 'great majority of children with epilepsy do not have

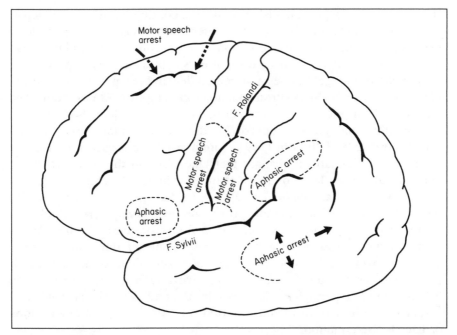

Figure 6.1 Diagrammatic representation of the left cerebral cortex showing areas of aphasic and motor speech arrest

specific language disorders'. Although such children are not the subject of this book I would suggest that the extent to which the language of children with epilepsy has undergone comprehensive language investigation is limited. Second, he proposed that 'genetic factors that predispose to specific developmental language disorder might also lead independently to epilepsy'; against this his data on children with a family history of language disorder showed a negative trend towards the development of epilepsy. His third hypothesis was 'that seizures may indicate abnormal brain development or damage' and, in favour of this, his data demonstrated a correlation between a history of seizures and antecedent abnormalities which might cause language disorder. This hypothesis implies that language disorders in childhood are not isolated abnormalities but 'associated with other kinds of cerebral abnormality or dysfunction'.

There have been no other studies which have tried to examine either the pathological mechanisms underlying the convulsive aphasias or their natural history. What follows is a discussion based on clinical observations of the five categories, discussed separately.

Convulsive status

Convulsive status may occur in children with various types of seizure: tonic/clonic, simple and complex partial, and myoclonic (Brown and

Hussain, 1991). Major convulsive status is a continuous state of epilepsy, with major convulsions lasting 30 minutes and no recovery of consciousness between seizures. The condition is more common in children, particularly those under 5 years of age, but no sex bias has been reported.

Epileptic discharges create an increased demand for glucose and oxygen in that part of the brain. Positron emission tomography (PET) has confirmed that there is an increase in cerebral metabolic rate, blood flow, oxygen consumption and glucose uptake by the human brain during seizure activity. Brown and Hussain (1991) summarised the stages of convulsive status and the metabolic changes that take place in the brain when the epileptic discharge lasts for more than 30 minutes. In children, various areas of the brain are highly susceptible to damage, and death may also result. Possible deficits include post-convulsive hemiplegia, which can occur when the child convulses for 2 hours or more. Unlike Todd's paralysis, which can occur with seizures of shorter duration and from which recovery will occur, this form of post-convulsive hemiplegia is permanent. Brown and Hussain (1991) gave a value of 11% for children having acquired hemiplegia as a result of convulsive status. Unilateral cerebral atrophy has also been reported on CT scans and temporal lobe damage is also common.

Where convulsive status is followed by prolonged coma then the child may recover with a range of deficits including speech and language problems. These may be associated with other cognitive, motor and behaviour deficits. The rate of recovery of speech and language after convulsive status has not been reported, but is probably dependent on a number of variables including the extent of the cerebral damage and the control of further seizures. Control of the epilepsy will be an important factor in prognosis because repeated convulsive status and subsequent coma are likely to add to such deficits.

Post-ictal phenomena

The occurrence of a transient motor weakness after an epileptic attack is one of a possible range of post-ictal phenomena. Such a weakness may last for a few hours or a few days and is known as Todd's paralysis. Other kinds of post-ictal phenomena are known, including a transient motor speech difficulty or other language disturbance. The essential features of a post-ictal phenomenon is that it follows seizures, and that the deficit is not permanent. Thus a post-ictal hemiplegia can be separated from a convulsive hemiplegia by its transitory nature. Where speech or language disturbance occurs as a post-ictal phenomenon, then it is important to establish the child's baseline language ability between attacks and to ensure that no significant communication or learning difficulties persist. In some children with evidence for only the post-ictal phenomenon, there might be an increase in paraphasic naming errors (see Cases 3 and 21). Even such transient deficits can have a traumatic effect on the child and he or she will require sensitive support. Other kinds of speech and language disturbances have been reported in children, including stereotyped and perseverated utterances, neologisms and dysarthria (McKeever, Holmes and Russman, 1983).

As a consequence of primary pathology

Few of the studies of traumatic aphasia have considered the implications of the occurrence of seizures. Aicardi (1990) reviewed the data on epilepsy in brain-injured children and recognised that a wide range of epileptic syndromes can occur secondary to cerebral injury. The incidence of epilepsy after head injury in childhood is not as well documented as in adults, but Ross et al. (1987) found at least 4 cases from 64 with epilepsy in the National Child Development Study follow-up data. After head injury, both early and late post-traumatic epilepsy can occur. Early post-traumatic epilepsy occurs in the first week of trauma and late post-traumatic epilepsy occurs at any time after that. Aicardi (1986) stated that the incidence of early seizures in children was probably higher than in adults and that at least 50% of cases occurred within the first 24 hours: most of these are focal, usually partial, motor attacks. However, Aicardi also reported that status epilepticus was much more common following head injury in children than in adults, and was highest in children under 5 years old. The risk of developing late post-traumatic epilepsy is said to decrease with time, and such seizures are more likely to be generalised.

The presence of cerebral tumour can also be a cause of epilepsy; cases in which epilepsy starts after the removal of a cerebral tumour have also been reported. Similarly, cerebrovascular abnormalities may lead to epilepsy or epilepsy may develop subsequent to haemorrhage of an arteriovenous malformation. Aicardi (1990) stated that 'the relationship between anatomical brain lesion and the functional phenomenon of epileptic seizures is poorly understood and extremely complex'. There have been various hypotheses concerning chemical changes, both at the cellular level and in the cerebral metabolism. Cerebral damage is usually increased when epilepsy occurs. However, generally, suppression of epilepsy may be obtained with anticonvulsants and/or neurosurgery depending on the case.

A number of the children reported in this volume have presented initially with seizures or later they have developed seizures as a result of primary pathology (see particularly Cases 3, 18, 19 and 21). In some of them (Cases 3 and 21), an increase in paraphasic errors in expressive language, and some fluctuations in receptive language, have been noted in association with episodes of seizures. In all of them, appropriate management of the epilepsy was an important part of their overall management.

As a feature of minor epileptic status

Although convulsive status is a life-threatening condition in which overt seizures are easily identified, minor epileptic status is often a hidden condition. Children may have periods of minor status for many years before they are diagnosed because the seizures themselves are more difficult to see. They may occur at night while the child is sleeping. When they occur during waking hours it may be thought that the child is not attending, not listening or has poor hearing, or that the child's fluctuating behaviour is 'just one of those things'.

The way in which minor epileptic status acts to cause cerebral damage is not clearly understood. It is recognised that a range of cognitive, behavioural and language deficits may occur, and usually these are fluctuating in nature. Where these persist for some time without being diagnosed, they may be dismissed as part of the child's background condition or even the child's fault. Where there is a high variability in some skills, particularly receptive language, which is not explained by hearing loss or general cognitive problems, then the possibility of minor epileptic status should be considered. If a series of formal language assessment results is available for a previous period of 1–2 years, then these should be looked at carefully to see whether they confirm the suggestion of a fluctuating disorder.

There should be a clear distinction, however, between those children with a long-term cognitive deficit associated with non-convulsive status epilepticus in sleep and those with the typical picture of waking minor epileptic (electrical) status with minute-to-minute variation in attention, often a 'groggy affect', continued myoclonic jerks and following this a variable motor disorder involving in particular bulbar movements.

As a psychological reaction to epilepsy

Little has been reported about the psychological effects of acute loss of communicative ability in children. One of the cases reported in this book (Case 9) clearly demonstrated a psychological reaction to his acute aphasia. When discharged home after 1 week in hospital for the treatment of cerebral abscess and mild aphasia, he was readmitted 48 hours later with complete loss of expressive speech. He was only communicating through writing. This was not the same pattern of presentation as his acute episode and led to further investigations on the supposition that he might have suffered a cerebrovascular accident subsequent to neurosurgery. However, all investigations were normal. Over the course of 3 days, through intensive support from the speech and language therapist, it became clear that he had many anxieties about returning to school. Three days after admission he began speaking again, and confirmed that he had not had aphasia but rather an elective mutism. He had thought he would be unable to cope back at school and had preferred readmission to hospital. With counselling and further support for communication skills, he did return, successfully, to his former school 2 weeks later.

It seems possible that if this kind of reaction to illness can occur in a child with a mild traumatic aphasia, then it is also possible in other situations, including as a reaction to epilepsy. The emotional support available to children needing it varies greatly from family to family and from school to school. A sensitive awareness of the stress suffered by children who experience speech and language loss is important for all team and family members. Children need to feel that there are people they can turn to for support in difficult situations such as the one described here.

Role of the speech and language therapist

The assessment of speech and language in a child with convulsive aphasia will depend to some extent on the duration of the problem. Where there is a post-ictal aphasia, the language disturbance may have passed before formal assessment can be arranged and only informal observations will be available. However, in such children it is important to carry out comprehensive assessment to ensure that residual language disturbances have not been overlooked, and to provide a baseline for assessment after any subsequent episodes. Similarly, in other convulsive aphasias, a number of baseline assessments will be helpful in determining any subsequent deterioration or in monitoring the effects of anticonvulsant medication.

As a minimum, an assessment of auditory verbal comprehension, naming and expressive language should be carried out. Where repeated assessments are required, ensure that this is within the bounds of test validity. If not, then a repeated series of informal observations, as carefully controlled as possible, may be used. An informal examination for use in these circumstances might include naming a set of pictures, selection of pictures to verbal command and story telling. The series of pictures should be large enough (i.e. over 25) to help rule out a memory component in subsequent reassessment.

Other aspects of the management of convulsive aphasias

In the diagnosis of convulsive disorders the use of EEGs plays an important part. An EEG may be recorded while the child is awake, or asleep, or even while the child is active over 24 hours or so, depending on the situation. Some convulsive disorders produce characteristic EEG patterns. In other cases it should be possible to identify whether the abnormality is bilateral or unilateral, symmetrical or asymmetrical, focal or diffuse. An analysis of these variables will contribute to the paediatric neurologist's management of the child.

The main aim of the treatment of epilepsy is to control any seizures. Aicardi and Chevrie (1986) stated that 'complete suppression of fits is obtainable in a majority of the childhood epilepsies' and further that a significant proportion will remit before adulthood. They reviewed a wide range of anticonvulsants and their side effects. They recommended the use of a single drug (monotherapy) wherever possible because this is simple for the child and family, and also avoids interactive effects. Where a child is maintained on anticonvulsants for some years then he or she should be monitored regularly. Where a child with convulsive aphasia is being monitored, then reassessment of speech and language should form part of that review procedure. It has been established that, in some children, the use of anticonvulsants may improve their aphasia (see Cases 13 and 19 particularly). Equally, the level of anticonvulsants needs to be carefully monitored to ensure that the dose remains at the right level for the particular child. This is done with a simple blood test.

There are other non-drug treatments for childhood epilepsy. The keto-genic diet is based on the suggestion that ketosis and acidosis produced by a special diet may help to control some types of seizures. The use of the diet requires daily urine testing and skilled dietetic support. The most obvious non-drug treatment for epilepsy is neurosurgery which may aim either to remove the origin of the seizures or to stop the discharges from spreading. Before surgery, an extensive range of psychological, speech, language and behavioural measures are carried out in order to predict as much as possible the effects of surgery on specific functions.

The schooling of children with epilepsy will depend on their educational needs. Many children will be well placed in a mainstream school. Others will require special educational placement, but not necessarily just because they have epilepsy. Similarly social activities need not always be restricted. The child's doctor should be consulted in respect of any specific concerns about activities either at school or at home.

Examples of children with convulsive aphasias

Case 16: a child with aphasia after convulsive status

This boy had a normal developmental history until he was admitted at the age of 8;3 years with a sudden onset of generalised grand mal convulsions. He was unconscious, but there were no focal neuro-logical signs. He responded to pain and not speech. CSF was clear and the white cell count was not raised. He had further fits and these were treated with rectal and intravenous diazepam. He was an only child, and his paternal uncle also had epilepsy. A CT scan was normal. He went into convulsive status and was transferred to intensive care. He was treated with intravenous diazepam, phenytoin, chlormethiazole (Heminevrin) and intramuscular paraldehyde, all of which failed to control his fitting. Mannitol was given and he was ventilated. The fits were finally controlled with thiopentone. An intracranial pressure monitor was inserted but the pressure was not elevated. A repeat CT scan was again normal. He passed a stormy 2 days in intensive care. Extubation was attempted but it was clear from the stridor that he had a lot of laryngeal ulceration and a tracheotomy was performed.

There were further periods of fits over the next 5 days as he gradually became more stable. However, he was withdrawn, made little eye contact, was unwilling to speak, had a weakness of the right arm and walked with a shuffling gait. His speech returned as a fluent aphasia: very long monologues irrelevant to time and place, interrupted with bursts of coprolalia. He had a severe receptive aphasia and was unable to localise sound, although brain-stem evoked auditory potentials were normal. He made a good gradual recovery and was discharged home on carbamazepine and phenytoin. Before this episode of aphasia he was right-handed but since the episode he has been left-handed. His expressive language continued to include paraphasic errors (Table 6.1). He received home tuition and continued to make progress with no further episodes of convulsive status. His major residual problems have been behavioural, particularly aggression, although he did eventually return to his previous school.

An example of his spontaneous language at the initial assessment, 1 month post-onset, shows his jargon aphasia which contained many neologisms (from a monologue while playing with toy cars):

'Leave me alone [unintelligible] eating [unintelligible] I don't know what [unintelligible] eat [unintelligible] I don't know what.

'I don't feel like that. I don't know. I feel sick. I'm barking, I know. The white [unintelligible] the same [unintelligible]. Your pandas, white pandas. That hand you like, it's the same. It's the same as the white pandas. I said about the......[hesitation] oh! Lead pandas. Up, up, yes, hot me. Hot boy. Really hold it. But I won't [unintelligible]

However, by 3 months post-onset this had resolved as the following example of the Dog Story shows:

'There was a little dog, carrying a piece of meat. He walked over the bridge. Looked over the bridge and saw his reflection. He thought he wanted that piece so he opened his mouth and dropped the fish and never saw it again.'

Table 6.1 Examples of paraphasias errors from the Word Finding Vocabulary Test* for Case 16

Assessment	Item	Response	Error type
2 months post-onset	Tree	Hat	Semantic paraphasia
	Knife	Nail	Semantic paraphasia
	Finger	Hand	Semantic paraphasia
	Snake	Snail	Semantic paraphasia
	Pear	Apple	Semantic paraphasia
	Bear	House/cow	Semantic paraphasia
	Chimney	Tree	Semantic paraphasia
	Kangaroo	Rabbit – not a rabbit	Self-correction
1 month later	Table	Chair	Semantic paraphasia
	Moon	Sun	Semantic paraphasia
	Snail	Snake/worm	Semantic paraphasia
	Coat hanger	Coat peg	Semantic paraphasia
	Feather	Leaf	Semantic paraphasia
	Goat	Cow	Semantic paraphasia
	Lighthouse	Windmill	Semantic paraphasia
	Anchor	Hook	Semantic paraphasia
	Parachute	Balloon	Semantic paraphasia
	Sleeve	Bat	Semantic paraphasia

* Renfrew (1977a).

There have been no subsequent episodes of convulsive status or aphasia.

Case 17: a child with aphasia as a post-ictal phenomenon

This boy was induced at term for rhesus incompatibility, and had an illness associated with seizures at 3 weeks of age. At 2;6 years he presented again with a generalised febrile convulsion. A CT scan at that time was normal. Focal seizures beginning on the right developed over the following 2 weeks and an EEG at that time showed a left occipital focus. He was treated with clomazepam. Over a period of 2 years this was withdrawn and there were no further fits. There was a recurrence of right focal fits at the age of 5;6 years which were diagnosed as myoclonic absences and focal attacks. These were associated with brief aphasic episodes and a deterioration in behaviour. His score on the TROG within 24 hours of one episode gave a z-score of -2 and he produced semantic paraphasias in expressive language. The episode lasted for less than 48 hours. He was treated with carbamazepine. An EEG at that time showed a bilateral abnormality. His hearing was normal. He was making little progress at school and was placed in a unit for children with behavioural difficulties at the age of 6 years. There have been no further episodes of aphasia, although his behaviour is still described as 'difficult' at school.

Case 18: a child with aphasia after seizures during recovery from neurosurgical treatment to remove a cerebellar tumour

This boy had a normal developmental history until admitted at the age of 10;10 years with a history suggestive of a mass lesion in the cerebellum. This was confirmed on CT scan as a mixed density mass and obstructive hydrocephalus. He underwent neurosurgery, ventriculoperitoneal shunting and resection of what proved to be a cerebellar astrocytoma, all of which was successful. He did well initially but on the third day after surgery he had a short series of right focal fits of unknown aetiology. A repeat CT scan showed no evidence of effect of the mass or bleeding. However, this incident left him with an acute aphasia and a degree of cortical visual loss. The latter was characterised by transposition of some images, either back to front or upside down. He showed little awareness of the visual loss. His vision gradually resolved so that 2 months post-onset it was 20/100. His hearing was normal. The major feature of his aphasia was a severe word-finding difficulty with some paraphasia (Table 6.2), and very little expressive language. Six months post-onset he had made good progress in all areas of skills and his recovery is shown in Figure 6.2. However, his Neale Analysis of Reading Ability was still below the 6-year level and his rate of

Table 6.2 Examples of naming errors from the Graded Naming Test* for Case 18

Post-onset	Item	Response	Error type
3 months	Turtle	Tortoise	Semantic paraphasia
	Trampoline	Tortoise	Perseveration
6 months	Kangaroo	Dog	Semantic paraphasia
	Buoy	Bucket	Semantic paraphasia
18 months	Buoy	Sandcastle	Semantic paraphasia
	Tweezers	Knife	Semantic paraphasia

* McKenna and Warrington (1983).

response on all tests was slow. He remained in mainstream school until secondary age when he was transferred to a placement for children with complex needs.

A sample of expressive language 3 months post-onset shows his non-fluent aphasia (from a description of a radio-controlled car):

> 'Well it goes quite fast and um…it goes left and right and forwards and backwards and it can go above ground.
>
> 'Well I actually have it on one of the school fields. When the school isn't [unintelligible] you know when there's nobody there.
>
> 'Well it's um… a radio controlled um…… well, sort of, well it's called a 'lunch box'. Well it's a um….yellow van and its um….shaped like a lunch box….sort of thing.'

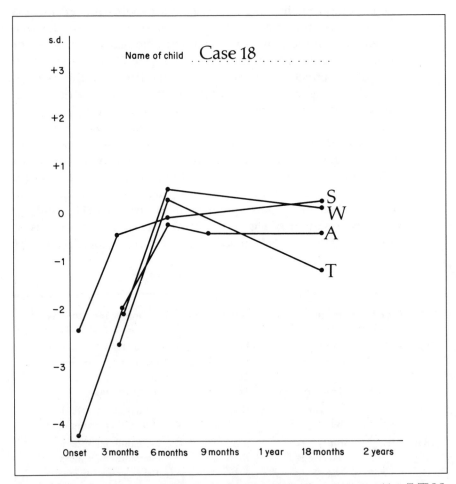

Figure 6.2 Profile of recovery of Case 18: A, auditory association; S, sentence repetition; T, TROG; W, Word Finding Vocabulary Test

Results from the story-telling test also show the same character-istics of a non-fluent aphasia and the graph of his recovery is shown in Figure 6.2:

Dog Story (6 months post-onset):
'The dog was carrying a piece of meat and he got to a pond and um.... he looked down and saw his reflection and he thought it was another dog and w..w..w..with a piece of meat and um...and he wanted that piece of meat which the dog was carrying as well. So he opened his mouth and he dropped the piece of meat into the pond.'

Case 19: child with aphasia and minor epileptic status

This boy (first reported in Lees and Urwin, 1991) was referred at the age of 8 years because there was some concern that his language skills, particularly his verbal comprehension, might be fluctuating. He had a congenital left hemiplegia arising from a large infarct in the region of the right middle cerebral artery and affecting a major part of the right motor cortex (confirmed by CT scan). He had no history of epilepsy or other developmental problems. He had first been seen by a speech and language therapist at the age of 2½ years. Although he had made some progress with speech and language development, he continued to have a severe language problem. He had been in a language unit since the age of 5 years.

His mother said that she had often been concerned about his hearing in the past and that he often appeared not to hear. However, all hearing tests were normal. Test scores of receptive language obtained since the age of 2;11 years using the RDLS and the TROG consistently gave standard scores below − 2. Apart from the motor signs on the left consistent with the hemiplegia, there were no other neurological signs. An EEG revealed an epileptic focus in the left temporal lobe, the region associated with the auditory association cortex and Wernicke's area. Anticonvulsant medication (carbamazepine) was started and gradually increased until blood tests confirmed a level within the recommended thera-peutic range. Repeat language testing did suggest an improvement in receptive language, which is shown in Figure 6.3.

Case 20: child with aphasia and minor epileptic status

This girl, the youngest of a family of three, was born after a full-term pregnancy, during which there had been some pain from 37 weeks onwards. Birth and early development were considered to be normal; birth weight was 4 kg; she walked at 14 months; her first words were at 2 years. There was a strong family history of migraine and allergies in both siblings. She began in mainstream school at

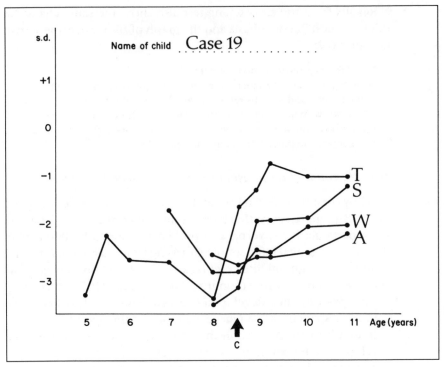

Figure 6.3 Profile of recovery of Case 19: A, auditory association; C, anticonvulsants started; S, sentence repetition; T, TROG; W, Word Finding Vocabulary Test

5 years and at that time speech and language did not cause any concern, although she was described as 'shy' and 'often on her own'. The school had open-plan classrooms and she did not appear to make any progress there, wandered around and often seemed distracted. It was at this stage that teachers and parents first began to ask questions about her comprehension and hearing. However, her hearing was normal when tested with pure-tone audiometry.

At 7;4 years a significant problem with verbal comprehension and expressive language was confirmed and she began sessions of speech and language therapy. Within a year she had been transferred to a school for children with speech and language disorders. Speech and language assessment from 7 to 10 years of age all documented the variability of her verbal comprehension and auditory verbal processing skills, particularly memory. She would sometimes score within the normal range on tests used and, on other occasions, there would be a drop of one or two standard deviations below the mean. There were no difficulties in articulation but language was described as short telegrammatic utterances. On other occasions she would use quite long phrases. Her expressive language was described as empty and immature but there were few grammatical errors. She was a good mechanical reader but comprehension was always poorer. At 8 years of age, her handedness was not clearly established. She was very slow to learn verbal concepts, such as time, and other aspects of more abstract language. Despite frequent mention of her variable performance in speech and language tasks, auditory verbal memory tasks and even in general responsiveness, it was not until nearly 3 years later that she was investigated further.

At the age of 10 it was noted that she was usually groggy on waking in the mornings. She had problems with fine motor function which made dressing difficult and, on some occasions, even basic washing and self-care seemed to take a long time and could be quite clumsy and disorganised. However, there was never any nocturnal incontinence. Her comprehension seemed to vary from day to day and she had particular difficulty with conversations with more than one person. Otherwise, physical and neurological examinations were normal. Her Full-scale WISC(R) IQ was 80, with Verbal IQ at 95 and Performance IQ at 68. An EEG recording at this time showed bilateral abnormalities with episodes of poly-spike and wave, and sporadic spike and wave over both hemispheres with no clear focus. It was concluded that the bilateral, atypical, spike and wave activity was suggestive of minor epilepsy which could well have been affecting her behaviour. She had a course of carbamazepine which had no effect and then phenytoin which did lead to some improvement.

She was placed in a secondary school for children with speech and language disorders at 11 years of age. The same kind of variability in receptive language and other auditory processing skills was also noted from time to time. Her language profile was rather patchy across expressive language skills with good scores for grammar but poor ones on semantic tasks.

Written language at age 8 years:
'I am seven yeurs old. I have Blue Eyes. I like wriTing and Drawing. When I grow up I will Be a nurse. I like going To scHool. a friend comes to play. I like to make THings at scHool.'

Written language at age 10 years:
'I am ten. long time from now I stopped being a Brownie. my eyes are blue. my best thing on a Saturday is watching neighbours. I hate getting stuck in sums. But I like doing seins and I like doing writing. my packed lunch is milk greek yogat pate roll. When I grow up I will be a zoo keeper looking after the Animals. I quite like Wednesday because there is swimming every Wednesday.'

Expressive language at age 8 years from The Bus Story Test (Renfrew, 1977b):
'Blew his whistle... trying to say stop.... but he just wouldn't stop.... nearly ran over a few people.'

Expressive language at 10 years (the Dog Story):
'There was a dog... who found a piece of meat. He went home to eat it. He went into the water and saw .... a flection... a reflection... and ... and when he saw that he thought that the other dog wanted his piece of meat. So he got his jaw open and tried to go for the reflection... but... but his bone fell in the water and was never seen again.'

Conclusions about this group of children with acquired aphasia

The group of children with convulsive aphasias is potentially a very mixed one. Only careful consideration of each case, including an understanding of the possible underlying mechanisms, will establish whether the child is presenting with a convulsive aphasia of the Landau–Kleffner type or another form of convulsive aphasia. However, clinical experience with a number of children with convulsive aphasia has lead to the observation that some professionals call any convulsive aphasia the Landau–Kleffner syndrome, and parents may adopt this exotic-sounding label to help their understanding of the child's problem. With the need to understand the subgroup contained by the term 'convulsive aphasia' better, more detailed case studies are required.

This group is also one in which we need more detailed longitudinal studies to evaluate: outcome in respect of the management of epilepsy; the provision of therapy and education; and the long-term prognosis of the various subgroups. At present, on the basis of the few cases seen, it can be concluded that for some children their aphasia improves with anticonvulsant medication. However, no clear pattern relating specific seizure disorders to particular anticonvulsants has emerged. Where a child with convulsive aphasia is going to be treated with anticonvulsants, assessment to monitor speech and language is important. In other children anticonvulsants may suppress the epilepsy, but speech and language will remain impaired. Such children need careful assessment to define their strengths and needs, so that a programme designed to maximise communicative potential, alongside their educational programme, can be implemented. Where epilepsy continues uncontrolled, it will be important to monitor any further effects this may have on speech and language and/or any response to other forms of intervention, including neurosurgery.

Chapter 7
Anomalous aphasias

Clearly, acquired childhood aphasia is a rare disorder and, equally, every child has a unique potential, although general developmental trends are recognised. It is not therefore surprising to find that it can be difficult to make generalisations about children with ACA. This is especially true of a subgroup of children with what shall be termed 'anomalous aphasias'. They are 'anomalous' in the sense that they do not easily fit the traumatic/convulsive division which was outlined in Chapter 1 and on which the other chapters have been based. Indeed, it is the very existence of this group that points to our ultimate need to develop a method of classifying ACA which not only is more satisfactory in coping with unusual causes but includes the linguistic perspective. Because of the individual nature of these cases, it is not possible to discuss neuropathology and natural history in general terms across the group. The cases will therefore be presented first and then the neuropathology and management implication of each one will be discussed.

Where traumatic and convulsive mechanisms combine

Case 21

This boy (first described by Lees and Neville, 1990) had a history of seizures from the age of 22 months. He had a congenital arteriovenous malformation of the left cerebral hemisphere in association with a capillary naevus on the left side of his face (his angiogram is shown in Figure 2.1). He had no evidence of large arterial disease. There was progressive hemiatrophy over the period of observation as revealed by subsequent CT scans. However, none of these scans showed evidence of cerebral infarction. The association of seizures and the absence of completed infarct all suggested that the probable pathology was small arterial cortical ischaemia. No further anatomical localisation was possible.

He was treated with anticoagulants. This was associated with a suppression of major episodes but not with complete suppression of epilepsy. On two occasions attempted withdrawal of anticoagulatants was associated with a relapse. Pure-tone audiometry confirmed normal hearing. He was 6 years old at the onset of an acute aphasia, with a right hemiplegia which resolved over 3 days. Aphasia persisted for 5 days. The return of language was characterised by a severe deficit of auditory verbal comprehension and jargon in expressive language, as well as some neologisms in naming tasks. This gradually improved and he did not receive speech and language therapy after discharge from hospital. He continued to make occasional paraphasic errors in naming tasks. Although he continued to make reasonable progress in his mainstream primary school, he did have particular difficulty with reading. A statement of educational need was made to include additional teaching and a 0.2. w.t.e. teacher was provided. Three years after the acute episode described he experienced some further episodes of disturbance in comprehension and expressive language which were characterised by a difficulty in auditory-verbal processing and increased phonemic paraphasias, but they were all under 24 hours in duration.

Story-telling data from the Farmer Story show how his expressive language improved over the first year of recovery from the initial aphasic episode to a rather non-fluent pattern, and the course of his aphasia is shown in Figure 7.1.

Farmer Story: 3 months post-onset

'Scratched the dog, barked at the donkey and frightened.'

Six months post-onset

'He had a farmer and he had a donkey and he had..... He was trying to put the donkey in the b.... barn and he said he thought and then he said. He was um ...... he thought a minute then he said if the dog bark the donkey go in the barn and he didn't. So he asked the tat .. cat to frighten him into the the um.....barn and he didn't. He asked the dog to bark. Then the cat frightened the um ..... into the barn.'

Nine months post-onset

'There there was an old farmer right and he had a donkey and he thought he could make him jump into the barn. So the dog bark and he and he didn't jump into the barn. Um... so the cat miaowed and then it still didn't jump into the barn. So so the farmer thought if if the er.... the cat scratched the dog and and the cat and then the dog barked and then the donkey jumped into the barn.'

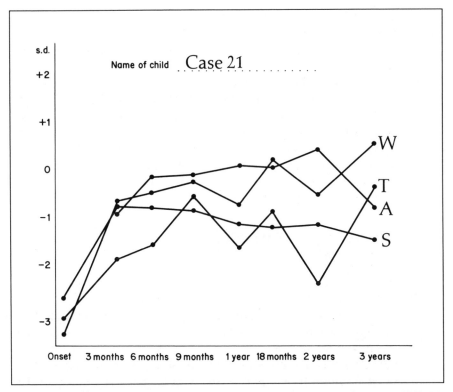

Figure 7.1 Profile of recovery of Case 21: A, auditory association; S, sentence repetition; T, TROG; W, Word Finding Vocabulary Test

Twelve months post-onset

'There was an old farmer and an old donkey and um...um... pushed him and pulled him. And he said the dog might have frightened him so he had a bark but he didn't move. So he asked the dog... the cat to as.. asked the cat to scratch the dog and .... then he said woof woof and he went into the barn.'

The Sturge-Weber syndrome is a capillary-venous malformation on the surface of the cerebral cortex and usually occurs in association with a facial naevus (port wine stain). These malformations are congenital in origin and consist of a large mass of enlarged and twisted vessels, which are supplied by one or more of the large cerebral arteries and drained by abnormal large cerebral veins. They are most commonly supplied by the middle cerebral artery and arise from a failure in the embryonic development of the cerebral circulation. In the most severe cases, the naevus may be quite large and extend from the face down the neck and arm. Epilepsy is commonly associated with this syndrome and the child may have a range of learning difficulties. However, in Case 21, the diagnosis of the Sturge-Weber syndrome was never confirmed and it seems best to regard this as an atypical case. The failure to confirm this diagnosis is not surprising. Isler (1971) reported the considerable variability in the syndrome.

The child described as Case 21 was also atypical in the way in which language disturbance occurred in association with the withdrawal of anti-coagulants, which is believed to signify further episodes of cerebral dys-function. These episodes appeared to have no effect on general learning and his IQ remained unchanged. The episodes were all quite small and were well controlled as long as both anticonvulsants and anticoagulants were given. In this case it is difficult to determine what separate contributions the vascular and convulsive disorders were making to the overall neuropatho-logy. Rather, it was possible only to observe the combined effect.

When language regression remains unexplained

Case 22

This boy was born at term from a pregnancy complicated by bleeding from 10 weeks onwards. However, his birth weight was 3.3 kg, and he was healthy and thrived with normal sucking and, later, chewing. His developmental milestones were initially normal: sitting at 6 months and two words with meaning at 14 months. He was just beginning to walk at this age. He had his measles immunis-ation and was ill for 2 weeks. He stopped walking and communicat-ing. For 6 months he was described by his parents as 'a different child'. He lost his previous communication skills, the words and the gestures, and seemed unable to understand what was said to him. In other respects he seemed normal, including symbolic play. His attention was poor and it was difficult to tell whether he was not attending or not hearing at times. However, when tested his hearing was normal.

He did not walk again until 18 months of age at which time he was still described as uncommunicative with poor attention. At the age of 3;4 years, both his receptive and expressive language were moderately impaired with standard scores of -1.5 and -1.8 respectively on the Reynell Developmental Language Scales (revised) (Reynell, 1985). Once again, his hearing was questioned in view of his variable attention but again it was normal. In view of the history of regression of language skills and the persisting communi-cation impairment, he was investigated for the Landau–Kleffner syndrome. An EEG and CT scan were both normal and he had never had any seizures. He received both regular speech and language therapy in a small group twice weekly and individual therapy once weekly for a year. At the age of 5 years he went into a mainstream primary class without additional support. Six months later he was said to be holding his own. His scores on formal language assessments were within the normal range for both receptive and expressive language. He was cooperative and had adequate attention although his school report stated that 'he can still present as being shy and timid'.

This child demonstrates some of the difficulties in diagnosing acquired language problems in childhood. His normal EEG and CT scan ruled out any significant cerebral pathology. However, he did undergo a marked change in behaviour and regression of communication skills which took over 3 years to resolve. When taking a detailed case history of any child presenting for speech and language assessment, the clinician should be alert for a history of unexplained periods of language regression. It is possible that, as in Case 22, these will remain unexplained. However, such children require careful monitoring to ensure that long-term problems do not persist.

Other conditions and syndromes in which the loss or deterioration of language skills in childhood may be one symptom

Children may present with a history of loss of language skills and, upon further investigation, it becomes clear that more than just language has been affected. The loss of language, or a more general deterioration in communicative ability, in a very young child can be the first sign of a more pervasive disintegrative disorder. When taking a case history in an older child with an acquired disorder, it may be observed that a reduction in communicative intent or the loss of recently acquired first words was noted early in the onset of the disorder. Reviews of studies of the effects of early brain damage in previous chapters have highlighted the vulnerability of language development in children with cerebral dysfunction. It is not therefore too surprising that children presenting with complex CNS dysfunction should also first show signs of loss of language. The importance of comprehensive multidisciplinary assessment to establish the range and extent of the child's problems and needs must be emphasised. Two such conditions are late-onset autism and Rett's syndrome.

Late-onset autism

There is continued debate about this condition. The syndrome of infantile autism was first described by Kanner in 1943. He presented a series of eleven cases (eight boys and three girls) and commented on five particular aspects of the development of these children. These were:

1. Inability to relate to other people as an early developmental difficulty.
2. Failure to develop normal communication skills.
3. A range of abnormal responses to things in the child's environment (objects and events) which appeared to be governed by an obsessive desire for sameness.
4. Some good cognitive abilities particularly with rote learning, memory and form boards.
5. Normal physical development.

The syndrome was further defined by Rutter (1978) who emphasised the distinction between general mental handicap and autism. He recommended the adoption of four criteria for the diagnosis of autism in children under 5 years: (1) onset of the disorder before 30 months of age; (2) specific impairment of social development not consistent with intellectual development; (3) a particular pattern of disordered language development that was also inconsistent with intellectual development; and (4) an obsession with 'sameness' which was demonstrated by stereotyped play, a resistance to change and unusual preoccupations. It was the insistence by Rutter that the onset of infantile autism could be anything up to 30 months of age that led to some dispute about the existence of late-onset autism. However, more recent research has advanced the case for separate recognition of such a syndrome.

Late-onset autism or distintegrative disorder was defined by Volkmar and Cohen (1989) as 'a type of pervasive developmental disorder characterized by a period of clearly normal development before age 2 followed by the onset of a marked loss of previously acquired social and communicative skills'. They stated that the typical course of the disorder was that the child's 'communication skills profoundly regress or virtually disappear' and that 'there is a marked deterioration of social and other skills', 'disinterest in the environment, and stereotyped movements' with motor skills and toileting being less consistently affected. The extent to which this late onset or disintegrative condition accounts for individuals with autistic spectrum disorders is not clear, but Kurita (1985) claims that it may have been up to one-third in one series.

There is 'no known unitary brain pathology common to all autism cases' (Gillberg, 1988) and the neurobiological basis of late-onset autism has not been satisfactorily identified. A number of mechanisms have been proposed, the most popular of which has been cerebral infection. Gillberg (1986) reported a girl who developed autism after herpes simplex encephalitis at the age of 14 years. Robinson (1988) reported 25 cases of children with 'acute disintegrative psychosis' who were investigated using auditory evoked potentials, CT scan and EEG. In all, 22 children, aged 2–5 years, had EEGs. In five of these the record was essentially normal. Of the remainder the abnormalities localised to the mid-temporal region in ten cases, temporoparietal in three and frontoparietal in four others. In all but four children there was some evidence of involvement of the other hemisphere with either contralateral spikes or generalised discharges. In five of the children, the EEG abnormalities were left-sided and in six they were right-sided or bilateral. He found no correlation between sex, laterality of handedness, age at onset or side of EEG abnormality, but admitted that the small numbers made this difficult.

As far as prognosis is concerned, Volkmar and Cohen (1989) identified 10 cases with 'late-onset autism' from a larger sample of 165 children who meet the behavioural criteria for autism, and stated that they made at best only a limited recovery. These ten cases, 6% of their total sample, were compared with two groups: autism of onset under 24 months and autism identified after 24 months but with no evidence of regression (i.e. a late 'identified' group). The 'late-onset' group had the lowest mean IQ. Differences in sex ratio and the presence of seizure disorder were not significant among the three groups. They concluded that once the condition was established, it was behaviourally indistinguishable from other cases of autism.

This of course raises the question of whether there is therefore any advantage in identifying these children as a distinctive group. Volkmar and Cohen (1989) agree that the distinction may be less important at the practical clinical level than in research studies. In the later situation, such cases may provide insights into the pathology of autistic disorders in the future.

The characteristics of the communication of these children have not been described in detail. The language disorders of 25 children with late-onset autism, aged 2–5 years at the time of exmination, were described by Lees (1988) (which were the same as the 25 children reported by Robinson, 1988). The language of the children could only be assessed using informal observations because of the severity of the communication, cognitive and social deficits. Results indicated that 14 of the children had no auditory verbal comprehension, that 10 had auditory verbal comprehension for single words only and that 1 (who was the eldest at onset) could comprehend two word phrases. Regarding expressive language, 14 had no expressive language, 10 others used single words occasionally and one used occasional two-word phrases and some echolalia. One of these children is described in Case 23.

Case 23

This boy was the only child of healthy, unrelated parents and had a history of a normal birth and delivery, after a normal pregnancy. He was said to have been developing normally, although first words might have been a little slow at 18 months of age. However, this might have been accounted for by his bilingual Spanish/English background. At 2;6 years he was reported to use two- to three-word phrases in Spanish. At the age of 3;4 years, concern was expressed by his parents and his nursery teacher that his development seemed to be slowing down. He gradually became uncommunicative and his behaviour regressed such that he became very difficult to manage, and engaged in repetitive behaviours. He was diagnosed as autistic. Nine months later his comprehension was at a single-word level and his expressive language consisted of a few echoed and stereotyped phrases. The deterioration in language continued, so that 14 months post-onset he had variable comprehension for single words and some echolalia. At this stage an EEG showed phase-reversing sharp waves in the left temporoparietal region. He did not have overt fits and his CT scan was normal. His behaviour remained difficult to control and there was no evidence of new learning in any modality.

By 18 months post-onset he had comprehension for common objects only and almost no expressive language. By 22 months post-onset, he appeared to have no verbal comprehension or expressive language. He scored at a 21-month level on the Symbolic Play Test (Lowe and Costello, 1976). An EEG at this time revealed phase-reversing sharp waves in both parietal regions, but more often on the right, and he was treated with carbamazepine. By 2 years post-onset he had no verbal comprehension or expressive language and his Symbolic Play level had fallen to a score equivalent to a 14-month level. He was then treated with a course of corticosteroids. Two months later he had improved so that he had situational comprehension and engaged in some brief symbolic activities with a symbolic play score at the 21-month level. However, there was no further improvement and former levels were not regained.

In many ways this child presented very like a case of the Landau–Kleffner syndrome with the additional loss of cognitive and social skills. Bishop and Rosenbloom (1987) recognised that 'differentiation between the Landau–Kleffner syndrome and infantile autism is occasionally problematic' and stated that although the majority of children with the Landau–Kleffner syndrome have normal social behaviour, some children do react badly to the experience of loss of communicative abilities. However, they are clear that 'these emotional disturbances are typically quite unlike the aloofness and avoidance of eye-contact found in autistic children'. The grey areas which appear between syndromes and disorders or the sense in which there seems to be some overlap has been a feature of my own clinical experience of children presenting with both acquired and developmental language problems. The distinction made by Bishop and Rosenbloom (1987) between the Landau–Kleffner syndrome and autism stresses the need for multidisciplinary assessment of children presenting with deteriorating conditions, so that a comprehensive profile of congitive, social and linguistic abilites can be prepared to enhance the accuracy of differential diagnosis.

Rett's syndrome

First described by Rett (1966, 1969), this syndrome is a severe form of learning disorder, the onset of which is between 1 and 2 years of age. Diagnostic criteria include: female sex (there are no known cases that are male), early regression of behaviour, social and cognitive development such that skills gained appear to be lost, signs of dementia, loss of hand skills and the development of hand-wringing stereotypies, the appearance of an ataxic gait and the deceleration of head growth. The most common misdiagnosis is infantile autism where difficulties of social and cognitive development are also seen, as are motor stereotypies such as hand-wringing. Children with Rett's syndrome do have stereotypical movements of the hands and poor social interaction. Gillberg (1988) pointed to the differentiation of Rett's syndrome as 'a striking clinical illustration of how the "autistic syndrome" will eventually turn out to consist of a number of syndromes with varying aetiology'. Evidence that the two syndromes, Rett's and infantile autism, can occur in one family was reported by Gillberg, Ehlers and Wahlstrom (1990). In an extended family, there were three female relatives with severe developmental disorders with onset in infancy: two with infantile autism and one with Rett's syndrome.

The usual course of the condition is that it follows a fairly normal first year of life, although motor milestones may be slightly delayed. Cognitive development is usually normal for the first 9 months, and then slows down before regressing in the second year. One of the most characteristic features of Rett's syndrome is the hand-wringing movements; the children also frequently put the fingers or hands in the mouth, and objects may also be mouthed persistently. A change from hypotonicity to hypertonicity in oral motor tone has been reported. This is said to be directly related to postural changes, fasciculating tongue movements and tongue deviation (more often to the left than to the right) (Budden, Meek and Henighan, 1990). These authors also assessed the communication development in 20 girls, aged 3–19 years, none of whom demonstrated a level above 20 months. The resulting clinical picture was of profound learning difficulties.

Case 24

This girl was born after a normal pregnancy and delivery at a birth weight of 2.8 kg. She was healthy and thrived. She was considered to be developing normally for the first 6 months of her life, although hindsight might suggest that she always reached motor milestones at the lower end of the normal age range. By the end of the first year she could feed herself with her fingers, could pull herself up to standing and cruise around the furniture. She would babble and had two or three clear words. At the time of her first birthday her development began to show a marked decline. She began to have periods of screaming and stopped using the few words she had learned. She gradually withdrew from social contact. She stopped babbling and was unable to feed herself. After about 6 months she was able to use her hands less and less, and stopped playing. She began to wring her hands almost continuously and seemed to have either her hands or toys always in her mouth, which became sore; she also dribbled. By the time she was 2 years old, she had ceased to engage in any constructive activity. Her communication was reduced to basic moaning and screaming. She was not mobile, continent or capable of any self-care. Also she did not learn any new skills. It is probable that this girl will remain severely communication and learning impaired.

Conclusions

These children point to the need to establish a comprehensive protocol for children with acquired disorders. Our classification systems are unable to account for all the cases we see. At present our understanding of language impairments in childhood, although progressing, calls for further research, the basis of which should be clinical observation, particularly of children with atypical conditions. If we are to learn from such children we need to develop and use a comprehensive assessment/investigation protocol which will at least mean that cases are reported consistently. This would help to facilitate across-child comparisons as well as providing a clear way of monitoring a child's long-term progress.

Because of the individuality of the children reported here, no conclusions about the course, prognosis and recovery of the group can be advanced. After all it is not one group, but rather a collection of subgroups and anomalous individuals. However, in general it can be said that where children present with regressive disorders, late-onset disorders or atypical acquired disorders in childhood, then those in whom the most skills are lost and in whom severe and uncontrolled epilepsy is a sequela probably have the poorest prognosis.

Chapter 8
Conclusions

There are few publications of this size devoted to the acquired aphasias of childhood from the perspective of a speech and language therapist. By now some of the reasons for that should be clear. ACA is a rare disorder and one which has attracted more attention from neurologists and psychologists in the recent past. Yet the speech and language therapist will potentially be called upon to work with more of these children. As an adviser to the College of Speech and Language Therapists, I have seen an increase in the number of enquiries about cases of ACA since the late 1980s. It is hoped that the discussion and cases presented here will help the clinician in the quest for 'How to know what to do' (Coombes, 1987).

There is, undoubtedly, a lot more we need to know, particularly about the relationship between developmental and acquired language disorders in childhood, the way in which improvement in function should be interpreted, and the relationships between neuropathology and language disorder subtypes. It is to be hoped that some of these questions might inform future reasearch.

For the clinician struggling with 'How to know what to do', the basic requirements of this client group are of immediate importance. As a result of considerable work by the speech and language therapy profession in the UK, professional standards were recently published (Smith, 1991). These standards cover the range of clients and working situations a speech and language therapist might be expected to deal with, including ACA. It is these guidelines that will form the basis of the first part of this chapter to highlight immediate practical issues of concern to speech and language therapists seeing this group of children.

Definition and description of acquired childhood aphasia

ACA is defined as a language disorder secondary to cerebral dysfunction in childhood, but appearing after a period of normal language development. The cerebral dysfunction may be the result of:

1. A focal lesion of one of the cerebral hemispheres or other area primary to language processing.
2. A diffuse lesion of the CNS above the level of the brain stem secondary to head injury or cerebral infection.
3. A diffuse lesion as in (2) but related to convulsive activity: as a consequence of convulsive status, a post-ictal phenomenon (Todd's paresis), as a consequence of primary pathology (e.g. malignant disease), as a feature of minor epileptic status or as a psychological reaction to epilepsy.
4. Unknown aetiology as in the Landau–Kleffner syndrome.

This definition aims to be inclusive of all known causes of ACA, both traumatic and convulsive. Furthermore, for the purposes of this definition, a language disorder is defined as a language profile that deviates from the normally expected profile of the child's peers in one or more areas, i.e. phonology, grammar, semantics, pragmatics, such that the child is disadvantaged in relation to his or her communication potential. It is therefore based on the premise that specific language deficits can be identified.

Aims and principles of the work of the speech and language therapist

It was the aim of the professional standards to set out the basic principles of working with each client group. Each chapter of this volume has included a section on the role of the speech and language therapist. Here are the principles that underly working as a speech and language therapist with this client group as a whole:

1. The child with ACA enters the social and educational context at a disadvantage as a result of the loss of previously held skills and abilities.
2. Although the usually understood model of ongoing development throughout childhood is still pertinent to this group, it must be viewed against a background of specific cerebral damage leading to significant deficits. These in turn may make a long-term contribution to a lack of progress in specific areas.
3. The complex nature of cerebral damage in ACA means that these children's needs are best served in a multidisciplinary setting.

4. The rate of recovery of a child with ACA will vary depending on a number of variables, including the severity of the initial damage and the stage of recovery that the child has reached, as well as the child's age and background. Therefore, the therapist's aims and objectives will require constant review and ongoing longitudinal assessment will be vital for appropriate placement.
5. Although the child may make a remarkable degree of recovery, present knowledge does not allow us to believe that complete long-term recovery to previously held levels is likely for the majority.
6. The clinician must constantly be aware of current research developments in this field and seek to relate these to her or his practice.
7. The child with ACA is a potentially different child to the one the family have always known and the therapist should seek to support and encourage appropriate communication within the family.

Referral to a speech and language therapist

There are a number of things that a speech and language therapist needs to know to be able to deal competently with a referral:

1. The neurological background of the child.
2. The child's developmental history, family history and history of previous educational attainment, where relevant.
3. Any change since onset of the disorder.
4. Where the referral is taken from another speech and language therapist, the previous history in resepct of speech and language therapy should be provided.
5. All the relevant members of the multidisciplinary team, educational, social, medical, therapeutic, psychological, should be informed of the therapist's conclusions regarding the referral.

For the future, the speech and language therapist should aim towards developing a comprehensive refferal system for all children with complex brain injury.

Assessment by a speech and language therapist

In each chapter some specific aspects of assessment have been addressed. Here the general conclusions that can be drawn about speech and language assessment are stated:

1. Few specific assessment techniques are available for this client group. Therefore the clinician needs to be informed about the use of the most appropriate ones for the child's age, background and needs.

2. A complex association of motor, cognitive, perceptual, emotional and communication problems can arise from brain injury in childhood and these make demands on the assessment procedure.

3. The deficits encountered in ACA are likely to require different assessment techniqes, both during the initial stages of often rapid improvement, as well as for long-term residual problems when the child's progress has reached a plateau.

4. These problems are uncommon and potentially complex. This may mean that the clinician will need to refer to a specialist colleague for advice during any stage of the management of the child.

5. It is important that an appropriate longitudinal reassessment protocol is used to map change, whether spontaneous recovery or as a response to treatment.

6. Assessment should seek to establish a comprehensive profile of the child's speech and language skills in a wide range of situations both formal and informal, including observations of the child in his or her environment and family setting.

7. Assessment should include: auditory–verbal comprehension; expressive language including word-finding ability; and should monitor the presence of jargon aphasia, phonemic and semantic paraphasias, the presence of errors including perseveration; and non-verbal communication.

8. Regarding the timing of assessments: during the first 3 months of recovery assessment should be more or less continuous. During the remainder of the first year of recovery assessments should be carried out regularly and at least every 3 months. After the first year of recovery long-term assessment plans should be for every 6 months to 1 year until the child leaves school or recovery is thought to have maximised. Research suggests that a few severely impaired children can show marked change in the long term and yet equally few recover fully, so speech and language assessment needs to identify and document both change and residual deficits as appropriate.

Intervention by a speech and language therapist

There are a number of general principles of speech and language therapy in ACA:

1. Remember to function as a member of a multidisciplinary team.

2. Be aware of the child's deficits, but always seek to maximise the child's communication skills by working through the child's strengths in an atmosphere of success.

3. Avoid unnecessary, prolonged and ineffective strategies which concentrate on the child's deficits so that the child's experience of failure becomes reinforced.
4. During the acute stage, concentrate on assessing the direction of change in communication skills and, where possible, building on residual skills, encourage the child to widen her or his communication.
5. During rehabilitation, be aware of the range of contexts in which therapy needs to be presented to achieve a well-balanced, diverse and relevant programme.
6. Do not ignore any long-term residual problems, which may be at a high level, and which require practical and functionally based therapy.
7. These children usually have complex educational needs which change during the course of recovery; therefore seek to represent the child's changing communication needs in the educational context and work within this setting.
8. With the more limited flexibility in learning after brain damage, remember that the child's communication needs are best served by a broadly functional approach which extends through all the child's learning contexts.

Discharge from speech and language therapy

Although few children may make full recovery to previously held levels, there will be the need to discharge children from the service. There are two principles the speech and language therapist should remember:

1. The changing nature of ACA warrants continued long-term review rather than premature discharge.
2. There should be an open re-referral system for those discharged.

Working with other professionals

This is essential for children with ACA because of the complex nature of their difficulties and the way in which these are managed by medical, educational and social services. Not every therapist works within an integrated multidisciplinary team, but it is essential to good speech and language therapy to be able to communicate with other professionals. Every therapist should seek appropriate ways of doing this and show some awareness of the contribution of other professionals to the needs of the child with ACA.

Because paediatric speech and language therapists deal predominantly with clients who have developmental disorders, they often find themselves poorly prepared to deal with the needs of the child with ACA. Where they are unfamiliar with the client group, they should liaise with a more experienced therapist. Where such a specialist does not exist within the locality, the national network of advisers to the College of Speech and Language Therapists may be approached.

A specialist speech and language therapist, for these purposes, should have had a period of experience with both language disorder and physical handicap in children, and be aware of the current state of research in this area when they have no direct previous experience with ACA. The College of Speech and Language Therapists also provides a network of relevant local or specific interest groups for those who want support and/or seek to learn more. Because of the paucity of information specific to ACA and the way in which it overlaps with other areas, clinicians should be prepared to liaise with those working in relevant areas, including adult aphasia, augmentative communication, special education, developmental language disorder and physical handicap.

Other aspects of the study of acquired childhood aphasia

Among the things that need to be finalised before completing this discussion of ACA, one outstanding matter, mentioned in Chapter 1, is that of classification. The traditional classification into traumatic and convulsive groups has been discussed. Although it is clear that this division does not account for all cases, it could be retained as a basic division provided it is recognised that anomalous cases do present from time to time. The question of what to call the various subtypes of aphasic syndromes is more problematic. It was concluded that neither the Goodglass and Kaplan (1972) nor the Rapin and Allen (1987) categories accounted for most of the children presenting with acquired aphasias (Lees, 1993). Yet many continue to use these categories and will do so until other more satisfactory systems are proposed.

In this regard, it is proposed here that the speech and language characteristics of children presenting with acquired aphasias should be reported as objectively as possible, so that the severity or mild nature of any aspect of the presenting disorder can be demonstrated. If the author of such a report claims that this child does, or does not, have any specifically named aphasic syndrome, according to whichever classification is used, then the reader can weigh up the evidence and agree or disagree. Where the child clearly does fit the criteria for a particular aphasic subtype, then this should be demonstrated in the report; where the child fails to meet any criteria this should also be clear. By strict reporting we should arrive at a more satisfactory understanding of the aphasic syndromes in childhood and the extent to which they can or cannot be categorised using the current systems.

Last we must address the problem of the evaluation of speech and language therapy in ACA. There have been no studies to date which have presented controlled data about the efficacy of speech and language therapy for these children. There have been a small number of single case studies (Gerard, Dugas and Sagar, 1991; Vance, 1991). Most studies which have said anything about the speech and language therapy received have provided insufficient details to draw any conclusions about its efficacy. Although not supporting Landau (1991) in his wish to see large numbers of randomised control trials in ACA, it is clear that we do need to address the efficacy issue.

There are a number of ways of evaluating outcome, but most will require much more detail about intervention than has previously been provided. Whurr, Lorch and Nye (1992), in a paper that analysed a large number of studies into the efficacy of speech and language therapy with adult aphasics using a method of meta-analysis, concluded that in this client group insufficient details were provided in most reported studies. They proposed some minimal criteria which would be required of future research if outcome measures are to be properly evaluated. These included specifications about the subjects, details of assessment, treatment and outcome. It is with future studies of ACA that we are now concerned and that is why Appendix II outlines the minimal information required to enable us all to gain a better understanding of the problems of these children. For the sake of each child who can say 'I just feel like I missed a big gap in my life', we must improve the way in which we study acquired childhood aphasia. I hope that this commitment will be the impetus of future clinical work and research.

Appendix I
Speech and language tests

The speech and language tests used to draw up the longitudinal profiles of the aphasic children given in this book have been used in previous studies (Lees, 1989, 1993; Lees and Neville, 1990). They were selected according to the following criteria:

1. They were available for use by speech and language therapists in general practice (both adult and paediatric services) and their administration was not dependent on a lengthy and complex training procedure.
2. They were designed to investigate a range of language problems, both receptive and expressive.
3. The time taken to administer the tests should be between 30 and 45 minutes, and be completed in one session, as this is realistic for routine clinical use.
4. The test material should be appropriate for children aged 5-16 years in terms of their content and, where possible, the availability of normative data.

The following language functions were tested, on the basis of previous reports of ACA in the literature.

Auditory verbal comprehension

The Test for Reception of Grammar (TROG) (Bishop, 1983) was used. This test of auditory-verbal comprehension of syntax was designed for use with language-disordered children aged 4-12 years. It consists of a picture book of 80 items. The pictures are coloured line drawings, four to each A4 size page. The items are grouped into 20 sections with 4 test sentences in each section, increasing in complexity from single nouns to complex sentences.

The examiner speaks the sentences in a normal manner, without undue emphasis or intonation, and the child responds by pointing to one of the four suggested pictures for that item. Older children may respond by saying the number 1-4 of the chosen picture. The examiner marks the chosen number on the response form, repeating the test sentence if necessary, and noting any hesitations, repetitions and self-corrections by the child. The child must produce four correct responses in each section to be credited as passing that section, and therefore with understanding at that syntactic level. The pattern of errors on this test can give some indication of the nature of the child's problems in auditory–verbal comprehension of either particular grammatical structures or a more general problem of understanding sentences related to speed and volume of auditory–verbal processing regardless of grammatical complexity. The test is norm referenced with both centile levels for age group, standard score interpretations being available.

Confrontational naming

Naming tests were used to assess the extent to which children made paraphasic errors when required to produce a specific target word. Because of the limited age range on most of the tests available, two tests were used for this. The first was used for the children aged 5-10 years, and the second for those over 11 years.

Word Finding Vocabulary Test (WFVT) (Renfrew, 1977a)

This test of confrontational naming was designed for children aged 3-8 years. It consists of 59 items, which are black and white line drawings on separate cards. The child is asked to name the pictures presented in test order. The child's response is noted as is any obvious evidence of hesitation, overt search behaviour, self-correction or no response. Equivalent age norms are available for both boys and girls Although an updated version of this test is now available (Renfrew, 1989) it differs from the 1977 version with regard to some of the items and the standardisation, and has not been used in these studies, all of which began before 1989.

Graded Naming Test (GNT) (McKenna and Warrington, 1983)

This test of confrontational naming was designed for use with neurologically impaired adults, but can also be used with teenagers. It consists of a booklet of 30 items, black and white line drawings, which the child is asked to name. The examiner records these responses noting any evidence of hesitation, overt search behaviour, self-correction or no response. Age norms and standard scores for 88 normal children aged 11-15 years were collected for this study and these are given at the end of this appendix. (Tables AI.1 and AI.2).

Association naming

The auditory association subtest of the Illinois Test of Psycholinguistic Abilities (ITPA) (Kirk, McCarthy and Kirk, 1968) was used. It is a test of association naming of 42 items. Normal data are available for children up to 10;6 years. The examiner asks a verbal question and the child's response is also verbal, e.g.

Q: A daddy is big, a baby is...?
A: Small.

A range of correct and incorrect responses is given with which to compare the child's response. Test items may be repeated and this noted, as should any evidence of hesitation, overt search behaviour or self-correction of error. Age norms and standard scores are available.

Short-term auditory–verbal processing and memory

Because selective deficit of repetition is a feature of some types of aphasia in adults, the ability to repeat sentences appropriately suggests that at least part of the auditory–verbal processing mechanism and short-term memory are functional. However, many young children do not like doing sentence repetition tests. Therefore, a sentence repetition test (subtest of the Neurosensory Centre Comprehensive Examination for Aphasia by Spreen and Benton, 1969) was used in which the child is asked to repeat sentences of increasing length from 1 to 20 words, in a total of 22 sentences. Hesitations, self-corrections and other errors are noted. The test is stopped after the child makes errors in two consecutive sentences. Normative data, including means for age and standard deviations, have been prepared by Gaddes and Crockett (1975) for children aged 6–13 years.

Expressive language

In order to make judgements about sentence structure, word order errors and fluency of expressive language, a language sample was required. Recognising the difficulty of eliciting expressive language in this group of children, a minimum of 10 sentences was used which were elicited in a story-telling situation according to the method recommeneded by Mandler and Johnson (1979). The two stories used were the Dog Story (11 episodes) and the Farmer Story (16 episodes). The complete texts are given here (and may also be found at the end of Lees and Neville (1990) and Lees and Urwin (1991)). Unfortunately norms are not yet available. However, the technique can be used successfully with most children of 6 years and over to elicit a short expressive language sample. The episode numbers refer to the major components of each story. A ratio of episode numbers (e.g. 8 out of 11) could be used to give an indication of how much of the story was accurately recalled. The stories should be told at an even pace, without any undue emphasis, but in as natural manner as possible. The child should then be asked to re-tell the story and can be cued if necessary. It is recommended that the child's response is tape-recorded for later transcription and any cues given should be marked. These stories can form a useful point of departure for subsequent conversation, particularly if the child was initially reluctant to converse spontaneously.

In addition spontaneous language samples of everyday conversation were collected from those children who could contribute more. All samples were tape-recorded and transcribed.

Other tests

For some of the cases reported here, other test results are given. This is usually either because they formed part of a broader study, as in the results for the children who survived prolonged coma in the study by Kirkham, Edwards and Lees (1990) in Chapter 4, or because their age at onset meant that other test material was more suitable. Among these other tests are the Symbolic Play Test (Lowe and Costello, 1976) and the Action Picture Test (Renfrew 1988), both of which are described in detail by Lees and Urwin (1991). The former is a non-verbal assessment for young children of their responses in four play situations. In the latter the child gives a verbal response to ten action pictures.

Complete Dog Story

Episode number	Story
1	There was a dog who had a piece of meat
2	and he was carrying it home in his mouth.
3	On the way home he had to cross a bridge across a stream.
4	As he crossed he looked down
5	and saw his reflection in the water.
6	He thought it was another dog with another piece of meat
7	and he wanted to have that piece as well.
8	So he tried to bite the reflection
9	but as he opened his mouth his piece of meat fell out,
10	dropped into the water,
11	and was never seen again.

Complete Farmer Story

Episode number	Story
1	Once there was an old farmer
2	who owned a very stubborn donkey.
3	One evening, the farmer wanted to put his donkey into the barn.
4	First he pushed him,
5	but the donkey would not move.
6	Then he pulled him,
7	but the donkey still would not move.
8	Next the farmer thought he could frighten the donkey into the barn.
9	So he asked the dog to bark at the donkey,
10	but the lazy dog refused.
11	Then the farmer thought that the cat could get the dog to bark.
12	So he asked the cat to scratch the dog.
13	The cooperative cat scratched the dog.
14	The dog immediately began to bark.
15	The barking so frightened the donkey
16	that he jumped into the barn.

Assessment procedures

In the longitudinal studies children were seen from acute onset of aphasia where possible. In those cases these tests were given when the child was considered to be neurologically stable which was usually within the first 5 days (although longer after head injury when a stable conscious level needed to be established), and repeated at 3, 6, 9, 12, 18, and 24 months post-onset where possible. In children referred during recovery, an initial assessment was made at that stage and the reassessment interval was dependent on the stage of recovery and where the child lived in terms of arranging repeat appointments or visits, but they were followed up to 24 months post-onset where applicable. Some children were referred more than 24 months post-onset with residual language deficit, and these generally completed only one language assessment. Incomplete follow-up was usually due to families moving away and being unable to make return visits or arrange home visits.

Assessments were carried out in a comfortable distraction-free environment. Individual assessments were arranged to take no longer than 45 minutes. All assessments were tape-recorded. All tests were carried out according to the procedures stated in the test manuals and results computed accordingly.

In addition raw scores from the standardised tests were changed to z-scores using the formula:

$$\frac{\text{Raw score} - \text{Mean score}}{\text{Standard deviation}} = z\text{-score}$$

Normal data for teenagers using the Graded Naming Test
(McKenna and Warrington, 1983)

This test was developed for the clinical assessment of adults with naming difficulties. Unlike many other tests, the items are not confined to common objects to ensure similar vocabulary for all subjects. It is well established that less frequently used names are more vulnerable to naming difficulties than the more frequently used and practised ones. Thus this test attempts to include some items that might be less commonly used in general vocabulary, in an attempt to take into account some individual premorbid differences and look at items on the fringes of the individual's naming capacity which might be more vulnerable. In the original study with adults, the standardisation sample was prepared from 100 subjects ranging from 20 to 76 years of age.

This test is commonly available to speech and language therapists, is easily administered, presented and scored. Although some of the vocabulary items were not thought to be commonly known by teenagers, it was thought to be a useful test of naming ability for the population aged 11–16 years and so preliminary measures of standardisation were sought.

The subjects for the standardisation were taken from two mixed comprehensive schools and two mixed junior schools in the south of England. All were state schools with classes of mixed sex, ability, race and socio-economic status. One of each type of school was situated in a city area and in a new town. A total of 88 children were tested and their age groups are detailed in Table AI.1

Table AI.1   Children tested on the Graded Naming Test*

Age range (years)	Girls	Boys	Total
11;0–11;11	14	14	28
12;0–12;11	13	9	22
13;0–13;11	11	11	22
14;0–14;11	8	8	16

*   McKenna and Warrington (1983).

The mean scores, standard deviation and range of scores for the age groups were calculated as shown in Table AI.2

Table AI.2   Mean scores, standard deviation and range of scores for 88 children tested on the Graded Naming Test*

Age range (years)	Mean score	Standard deviation	Range of scores
11;0–11;11	9.6	5	3–19
12;0–12;11	10.5	2.72	6–15
13;0–13;11	14.4	3.2	10–20
14;0–14;11	12.2	4.8	3–22

*   McKenna and Warrington (1983).

Although these data require supplementation, particularly at the higher age range, it does serve as a basis for using this test with teenagers who have specific naming problems. Observations from the responses of this normal sample, which have proved useful when seeing aphasic teenagers, include the following.

Order of difficulty of test items for normal children

McKenna and Warrington (1983) discussed the order of difficulty of the items in the test regarding their normal adult population. The tests are said to be arranged in order of difficulty for normal adults. It is therefore interesting to note that this order of difficulty was not the same for the normal children in this sample. They found items such as 'trampoline' (17), 'shuttlecock' (19) and 'leotard' (23) much easier to recall than 'periscope' (12), 'blinkers' (14) and 'monocle' (15). These appear to be easier for adults according to the test manual. However, there was one item that was almost unknown to all the children: 'sporran' (8). These observations would appear to be related to the children's experience of these items.

Cueing techniques used by normal children

Most of the children found the test situation quite demanding, although all were happy to comply. However, almost all of them showed evidence of word-finding difficulty under the stress of the test situation. This could be described as the 'tip-of-the-tongue' phenomenon. When this occurred they used a range of self-cueing strategies which have been arranged in order of frequency of use:

1. Gestural cue: making a movement indicative of the item.
2. Verbal description cue: using a phrase of sentence to describe the item.
3. Negative statement: saying 'it's not a ..'.
4. Phonemic cue: saying 'it begins with .....'.

These observations are of interest regarding therapy with aphasic children because the teaching of such strategies often forms the cornerstone of therapy for children with word-finding problems.

Naming errors in normal children

McKenna and Warrington (1983) also discuss the naming errors found in their normal sample. They are very similar to those observed from this normal sample of teenagers. The children differed from the aphasic children regarding the errors they made in that only one child in the normal group produced a paraphasic error ('cuttleshock' for 'shuttlecock') which she was unable to self-correct. Uncorrected paraphasias were the main persisting errors in the naming of the aphasic children.

Appendix II
Protocol for the study of ACA

Proposed protocol for the study of children with acquired aphasias

1. Basic information:
   Name (or initials or case identification number):
   Date of birth:
   Sex:
   Age at onset (or at presentation of this episode):

2. Case history, including:
   Pre-existing abnormalities including seizures, history of language development, any previous neurological problems

3. Family history

4. A statement of the aetiology

5. A clinical neurological summary with localisation of the deficits as far as possible

6. Positive statement of investigations including CT scan, EEG, angiogram etc., with dates of each where applicable. Where possible lesions on scans should be rated according to the criteria proposed by Vargha-Khadem, O'Gorman and Watters (1985)

7. Follow-up information: note, always report details in respect of time since onset

8. Treatment given: medical treatment and therapy, including drugs, length of treatment period, number of sessions, length of sessions,

type of treatment, whether therapy provided by qualified therapist, teacher, family member or volunteer

9. An appropriate test of hearing

10. Information about pre- and post-onset cognitive function; Full-scale WISC or equivalent, details of school attended and any special educational needs

11. Language test results:
For each assessment the test results should be recorded as both raw scores and z-scores
Where longitudinal test data are available it should be displayed on graphs where the x-coordinate is time (e.g. months since onset) and the y-coordinate is the z-score (both above and below the mean) as given in the case examples in the text
As a minimum, formal language tests of auditory–verbal comprehension and confrontational naming should be used
Additionally a qualitative analysis of responses for the language tests should be given according to the following code:
  B   response after a delay (up to approximately 10 seconds)
  C   examiner repeated instructions due to time lag or at child's request
  Ci child repeated instructions to self
  D   self-corrected response after:
     i   misidentification
     ii extended description
     iii semantic paraphasia
     iv phonemic paraphasia
     v   neologism
     vi perseveration
     vii other
The number of these types of responses should be noted as follows:
$B \times 4$ (or B/4), which means that four delayed responses were produced on a given test
Where the language data includes naming errors they are to be coded as follows:
  sp = semantic paraphasia
  pp = phonemic paraphasia
  ng = neologism

12. Transcriptions of language samples: either spontaeous language or from story telling

References

AGOSTINI, M. DE and KREMIN, H. (1986). Homogeneity of the syndrome of acquired aphasia in childhood revisited: Case study of a child with transcortical aphasia. *Journal of Neurolinguistics*, **2**, 179-187.

AICARDI, J. (ed.) (1986). Post-traumatic epilepsy. In: *Epilepsy in Children*. New York: Raven Press.

AICARDI, J. (1990). Epilepsy in brain injured children. *Developmental Medicine and Child Neurology*, **32**, 191-202.

AICARDI, J. and CHEVRIE J.J. (1986). Children with Epilepsy. In: N. Gordon, and I. McKinlay (eds), *Neurologically Handicapped Children: Treatment and Management*. Oxford: Blackwell.

ALAJOUANINE, T. and LHERMITTE, F. (1965). Acquired aphasia in children. *Brain*, **88**, 653-662.

ARAM, D. (1991a). Test battery for language and speech assessment. In: I.P. Martins, A. Castro-Caldas, H.R. Van Dongen, and A. Van Hout (eds), *Acquired Aphasia in Children: Acquisition and Breakdown of Language in the Developing Brain*. Dordrecht: Kluwer Academic Publications (in cooperation with NATO Scientific Affairs Division).

ARAM, D. (1991b). Scholastic achievement after early brain lesions. In: I.P. Martins, A. Castro-Caldas, H.R. Van Dongen and A. Van Hout (eds), *Acquired Aphasia in Children: Acquisition and Breakdown of Language in the Developing Brain*. Dordrecht: Kluwer Academic Publications (in cooperation with NATO Scientific Affairs Division).

ARAM, D.M. and EKELMAN, B.L. (1988a). Scholastic aptitude and achievement among children with unilateral brain lesions. *Neuropsychologia*, **26**, 903-916.

ARAM D.M. and EKELMAN, B.L. (1988b). Auditory temporal perception of children with left or right brain lesions. *Neuropsychologia*, **26**, 931-935.

ARAM, D.M., EKELMAN, B.L. and GILLESPIE, L.L. (1989). Reading and lateralised brain lesions in children. In: K. Von Euler (ed.), *Developmental Dyslexia and Dysphasia*. London: Macmillan.

ARAM, D.M., EKELMAN, B.L. and WHITAKER, H.A. (1987). Lexical retrieval in left and right brain lesioned children. *Brain and Language*, **27**, 75-100.

ARAM, D.M., ROSE, D.F., REKATE, H.L. and WHITAKER, H.A. (1983). Acquired capsular/striatal aphasia in childhood. *Archives of Neurology*, **40**, 614-617.

BAX, M.C.O. (1964). Terminology and classification of cerebral palsy. *Developmental Medicine and Child Neurology*, **6**, 296-297.

BEAMANOIR, A. (1985). The Landau-Kleffner Syndrome. In: J. Roger, C. Dravet, M. Bureua, F.E. Dreifuss, and P. Wolf (eds), *Epileptic Syndromes in Infancy, Childhood and Adolescence*. Paris: John Libbey, Eurotex.

BISHOP, D.V.M. (1982). Comprehension of spoken, written and signed sentences in childhood language disorders. *Journal of Child Psychology and Psychiatry*, **23**(1), 1-20.

BISHOP, D.V.M. (1983). *The Test for Reception of Grammar*. Published by the author at the MRC Applied Psychology Research Unit, 15 Chaucer Road, Cambridge CB2 2EF.

BISHOP, D.V.M. (1985). Age of onset and outcome in 'Acquired Aphasia with Convulsive Disorder' (Landau-Kleffner Syndrome). *Developmental Medicine and Child Neurology*, **27**, 705-712.

BISHOP, D.V.M. (1988). Language development after focal brain damage. In: D. Bishop, and K. Mogford (eds), *Language Development in Exceptional Circumstances*. Edinburgh: Churchill Livingstone.

BISHOP, D. and MOGFORD, K. (eds) (1988). *Language Development in Exceptional Circumstances*. Edinburgh: Churchill Livingstone.

BISHOP, D. and ROSENBLOOM, L. (1987). Classification of childhood language disorders. In: W. Yule, and M. Rutter (eds), *Language Development and Disorders*. Oxford: Blackwell Scientific Publications/Mac Keith Press.

BRIMMER, M.A and DUNN, L.A. (1973). *English Picture Vocabulary Test*. Gloucester: Education Evaluation Enterprises.

BRINDLEY, C., CAVE, D., CRANE, S., LEES, J. and MOFFAT, V. (1993). *The Paediatric Oral Skills Package*, in press. London: Whurr Publishers.

BROOKHOUSER, P.E., AUSLANDER, M.C. and MESKAN, M.E. (1988). The pattern and stability of post-meningitic hearing loss in children. *The Laryngoscope*, **98**, 940-947.

BROWN, J.K. and HUSSAIN, I.H.M.I. (1991). Status Epilepticus I: Pathogenesis. *Developmental Medicine and Child Neurology*, **33**, 3-17.

BUDDEN, S., MEEK, M. and HENIGAN, C. (1990). Communication and oral-motor function in Rett Syndrome. *Developmental Medicine and Child Neurology*, **32**, 51-55

BZOCH, K.R. and LEAGUE, R. (1970). *The Receptive and Expressive Emergent Language Scale*. Baltimore: University Park Press.

CARTER, R.L., HOHENGGER, M.K. and SATZ, P. (1982). Aphasia and speech organisation in children. *Science*, **218**, 797-799.

CHADWICK, O., RUTTER, M., THOMPSON, J. and SCHAFFER, D. (1981). Intellectual performance and reading skills after localised head injury in childhood. *Journal of Child Psychology and Psychiatry*, **22**, 117-139.

COLLIGNON, R., HECAEN, H. and ANGELERGUES, G. (1968). A propos de 12 cas d'aphasie acquise de l'enfant. *Acta Neurologica et Psychiatrica Belgica*, **68**, 245-277.

COOMBES, K. (1987). Speech Therapy. In: W. Yule, and M. Rutter (eds), *Language Development and Disorders*. Oxford: Blackwell Scientific Publications/Mac Keith Press.

COOPER, J.A. and FERRY, P.C. (1978). Acquired auditory verbal agnosia and seizures in childhood. *Journal of Speech and Hearing Disorders*, **43**, 176-184.

CORBETT, J. (1985). Epilepsy as part of a handicapping condition. In: E. Ross, and E. Reynolds (eds), *Paediatric Perspectives on Epilepsy*. Chichester: J Wiley & Sons.

CROSS, J.A. and OZANNE, A.E. (1990). Acquired childhood aphasia: assessment and treatment. In: B.E. Murdoch (ed.), *Acquired Neurological Speech/Language Disorders in Childhood*. London: Taylor & Francis.

CRYSTAL, D., FLETCHER, P. and GARMAN, M. (1989). *The Grammatical Analysis of Language Disability*, 2nd edn. London: Whurr Publishers.

DE RENZI, E. and VIGNOLO, L. (1962). The Token Test; a sensitive test to detect disturbances in aphasics. *Brain*, **85**, 665–678.

DE WIJNGAERT, E. (1991). The Landau–Kleffner syndrome: Rehabilitation.   In: I.P. Martins, A. Castro-Caldas, H.R. Van Dongen and A. Van Hout (eds), *Acquired Aphasia in Children: Acquisition and Breakdown of Language in the Developing Brain*. Dordrecht: Kluwer Academic Publications (in cooperation with NATO Scientific Affairs Division).

DENNIS, M. (1980). Strokes in childhood I: Communicative intent, expression and comprehension after left hemisphere arteriopathy in a right handed nine year old. In: *Language Development and Aphasia*. New York: Academic Press.

DEONNA, T., BEAUMANOIR, A., GAILLARD, F. and ASSAL, G. (1977). Acquired aphasia in childhood with seizure disorder; a heterogeneous syndrome. *Neuropediatrics*, **8**, 263–273.

DI SIMONI, F. (1978). *The Token Test for Children*. Boston: Teaching Resources Corporation.

DUGAS, M., GRENET, P., MASSON, M., MIALET, J.P. and JAQUET, G. (1976). Aphasie de l'enfant avec epilepsie; evolution regressive sous traitment antiepileptique. *Revue Neurologique (Paris)*, **132**, 489–493.

DUGAS, M., GERARD, C.L., FRANC, S. and SAGAR, D. (1991). Natural History, course and prognosis of the Landau and Kleffner Syndrome. In: I.P. Martins, A. Castro-Caldas, H.R. Van Dongen and A. Van Hout (eds), *Acquired Aphasia in Children: Acquisition and Breakdown of Language in the Developing Brain*. Dordrecht: Kluwer Academic Publications (in cooperation with NATO Scientific Affairs Division).

DULAC, O., BILLARD, C. and ARTHUIS, M. (1983). Aspects electrocliniques et evolutifs de l'epilepsie dans le syndrome aphasie-epilepsie. *Archives Françaises de Pediatrie*, **40**, 299–308.

EISELE, J.A. (1991). Selective deficits in language comprehension following early left and right hemisphere damage. In: I.P. Martins, A. Castro-Caldas, H.R. Van Dongen and A. Van Hout (eds), *Acquired Aphasia in Children: Acquisition and Breakdown of Language in the Developing Brain*. Dordrecht: Kluwer Academic Publications (in cooperation with NATO Scientific Affairs Division).

ENDERBY, P. (1983). *The Frenchay Dysarthria Test*. Windsor: NFER-Nelson.

EWING-COBBS, L., FLETCHER, J.M., LANDRY, S.H. and LEVIN, H.S. (1985). Language disorders after paediatric head injury. In: *Speech and Language Evaluation in Neurology; Childhood Disorders*. New York: Grune & Stratton.

FREUD, S. (1897). *Die Infantile Cerebrallaehmung*. (Infantile cerebral paralysis.) Translated by L.A. Russin (1968). Coral Gables: University of Miami Press.

GADDES, W.H. and CROCKETT, D.J. (1975). The Spreen–Benton aphasia tests: normative data as a measure of language development. *Brain and Language*, **3**, 257–280.

GERARD, C.L., DUGAS, M. and SAGAR, D. (1991). Speech therapy in Landau and Kleffner Syndrome. In: I.P. Martins, A. Castro-Caldas, H.R. Van Dongen and A. Van Hout (eds), *Acquired Aphasia in Children: Acquisition and Breakdown of Language in the Developing Brain*. Dordrecht: Kluwer Academic Publications (in cooperation with NATO Scientific Affairs Division).

GERMAN, D.J. (1986). *National College of Education Test of Word Finding (TWF)*. Allen, TX: DLM Teaching Resources.

GILLBERG, C. (1986). Onset at age 14 of a typical autistic syndrome. A case report of a girl with herpes simplex encephalitis. *Journal of Autism and Developmental Disorders*, **16**, 569–575.

GILLBERG, C. (1988). The neurobiology of infantile autism. *Journal of Child Psychology and Psychiatry*, **29** (3), 257-266.

GILLBERG, C., EHLERS, S. and WAHLSTROM, J. (1990). The syndromes described by Kanner and Rett-Hagberg: Overlap in an extended family. *Developmental Medicine and Child Neurology*, **32**, 258-266.

GOODING, C.A., BRASCH, R.C., LALLEMAND, D.P., WESBEY, G.E. and BRANDT-ZAWADZKI, M.N. (1984). Nuclear magnetic resonance imaging of the brain in children. *Journal of Pediatrics*, **104**, 509-515.

GOODGLASS, H. and KAPLAN, E. (1972). *The Assessment of Aphasia and Related Disorders*. Philadelphia: Lea and Febiger.

GRIFFITHS, R. (1954). *The Abilities of Babies*. Windsor: NFER-Nelson.

GRIFFITHS, R. (1970). *The Abilities of Young Children*. Windsor: NFER-Nelson.

GUTTMAN, E. (1942). Aphasia in children. *Brain*, **65**, 205-219.

HAYNES, C. (1992). A longitudinal study of language impaired children from a residential school. In: P. Fletcher, and D. Hall (eds), *Specific Speech and Language Disorders in Children*. London: Whurr Publishers.

HECAEN, H. (1976). Acquired aphasia in children and the ontogenesis of hemispheric specialization. *Brain and Language*, **3**, 114-134.

HOWARD, D., PATTERSON, K.E., FRANKLIN, S., ORCHARD-LISLE, V.M. and MORTON, J. (1985). Treatment of word retreival deficits in aphasia; a comparision of two therapy methods. *Brain*, **108**, 817-829.

HUDSON, L.J. (1990). Speech and language disorders in childhood brain tumours. In: B.E. Murdoch (1990) (ed.) *Acquired Neurological Speech/Language Disorders in Childhood*. London: Taylor and Francis.

HUDSON, L.J., MURDOCH, B.E. and OZANNE, A.E. (1989). Posterior fossa tumours in childhood: associated speech and language disorders post-surgery. *Aphasiology*, **3**, 1-18.

HUSKISSON, J.A. (1973). Acquired receptive language difficulties in childhood. *British Journal of Disorders of Communication*, **8**, 54-63.

ISLER, W. (1971). *Acute Hemiplegias and Hemisyndromes in Childhood*. Spastics International Medical Publications. London: William Heinemann Medical Books.

JOHNSON, D. and ROETHIG-JOHNSON, K. (1987). Stopping the slide of head injured children. *Special Children*, November 1987, 18-20.

JORDAN, F.M., OZANNE, A.E. and MURDOCH, B.E. (1988). Long-term speech and language disorder subsequent to closed head injury in children. *Brain Injury*, **2**, 179-185.

KANNER, L. (1943). Autistic disturbance of affective contact. *Nervous Child*, **2**, 179-185.

KELLY, J.J., MELLINGER, J.F. and SUNDT, T.M. (1978). Intracranial arteriovenous malformations in childhood. *Annals of Neurology*, **3**, 338-343.

KIRK, S.A, McCARTHY, J.J. and KIRK, W.D. (1968). *The Illinois Test of Psycholinguistic Abilities*. Illinois: University of Illinois.

KIRKHAM, F., EDWARDS, M. and LEES, J. (1990). Recovery of congitive and language skills after prolonged coma in childhood. Paper presented at the IVth International Aphasia Rehabilitation Congress, 4-6 September 1990, Edinburgh.

KNOWLES, W. and MASIDLOVER, M. (1982). *The Derbyshire Language Scheme*. Available from: The Education Office, Grosvenor Road, Ripley, Derbyshire.

KURITA, H. (1985). Infantile autism with speech loss before the age of thirty months. *Journal of the American Academy of Child Psychiatry*, **24**, 191-196.

LANDAU, W.M. (1991). The conception and embarrassing birth of an eponym. In I.P. Martins, A. Castro-Caldas, H.R. Van Dongen, and Van Hout, A. (eds), *Acquired Aphasia in Children: Acquisition and Breakdown of Language in the Developing Brain*. Dordrecht: Kluwer Academic Publications (in cooperation with NATO Scientific Affairs Division).

LANDAU, W.M. and KLEFFNER, F. (1957). Syndrome of acquired aphasia and convulsive disorder in children. *Neurology*, 7, 523-530.

LEA, J. (1965). A language scheme for children suffering from receptive aphasia. *Speech Pathology and Therapy*, 8, 56-68.

LEA, J. (1970). *The Colour Pattern Scheme; a method of remedial language teaching*. Available from Moor House School, Oxted, Surrey.

LEA, J. (1979). Language development through the written word. *Child Care Health and Development*, 5, 69-74.

LEES, J.A. (1988). What does acquired childhood aphasia say to late onset autism? Paper presented at the 16th International Study Group on Child Neurology and Cerebral Palsy, 26-30 September 1988, Cambridge.

LEES, J.A. (1989). *A Linguistic Investigation of Acquired Childhood Aphasia*. Unpublished MPhil thesis: City University, London.

LEES, J.A. (1993). Differentiating language disorder subtypes in acquired childhood aphasia. *Aphasiology*, in press.

LEES, J.A. and NEVILLE, B.G.R. (1990). Acquired aphasia in childhood: case studies of five children. *Aphasiology*, 4, 463-478.

LEES, J. and URWIN, S. (1991). *Children with Language Disorders*. London: Whurr Publishers.

LEITER, R. (1969). *Leiter International Performance Scale*. Chicago: Stoelting.

LESSER, R. (1978). *Linguistic Investigation of Aphasia*. London: Edward Arnold.

LESSER, R.P., LUDERS, H., MORRIS, H.H., et al. (1986). Electrical stimulation of Wernicke's area interferes with comprehension. *Neurology*, 36, 658-662.

LEVIN, H.S., MADDISON, C.F., BAILEY, C.B., et al. (1983). Mutism after closed head injury. *Archives of Neurology*, 40, 601-606

LOONEN, C.B. and VAN DONGEN, H.R. (1990). Acquired childhood aphasia: Outcome one year after onset. *Archives of Neurology*, 47, 1324-1328.

LOWE, M. and COSTELLO, A.J. (1976). *The Symbolic Play Test*. Windsor: NFER-Nelson.

McCABE, R.J.R. and GREEN, D. (1987). Rehabilitating severely head-injured adolescents: three case studies. *Journal of Child Psychology and Psychiatry*, 28, 111-126.

McKEEVER, M., HOLMES, G.L. and RUSSMAN, B.S. (1983). Speech abnormalities in seizures: A comparison of absence and partial complex seizures. *Brain and Language*, 19, 25-32.

McKENNA, P. and WARRINGTON, E. (1983). *The Graded Naming Test*. Windsor: NFER-Nelson.

McKINNEY, W. and McGREAL, D.A. (1974). An aphasic syndrome in children. *Canadian Medical Association Journal*, 110, 637-639.

MANDLER, J.M. and JOHNSON, N.S. (1977). Remembrance of things parsed: story structure and recall. *Cognitive Psychology*, 8, 111-151.

MANTOVANI, J.F. and LANDAU, W.M. (1980). Acquired aphasia with convulsive disorder: course and prognosis. *Neurology*, 30, 524-529.

MARESCAUX, C., HIRSCH, E., FINK, S., et al. (1990). Landau–Kleffner Syndrome: A Pharmacologic Study of Five Cases. *Epilepsia*, 31, 768-777.

MARSHALL, J.C. (1986). The description and interpretation of aphasic language disorder. *Neuropsychologia*, 24, 5-24.

MARTINS, I.P. and FERRO, J.M. (1987). Acquired conduction aphasia in a child. *Developmental Medicine and Child Neurology*, 29, 529-540.

MARTINS, I.P. and FERRO, J.M. (1991). Recovery from aphasia and lesions size in the temporal lobe. In: I.P. Martins, A. Castro-Caldas, H.R. Van Dongen, and A. Van Hout (eds), *Acquired Aphasia in Children: Acquisition and Breakdown of Language in the Developing Brain*. Dordrecht: Kluwer Academic Publications (in cooperation with NATO Scientific Affairs Division).

MARTINS, I.P., FERRO, J.M. and TRINDADE, A. (1987). Acquired crossed aphasia in a child. *Developmental Medicine and Child Neurology*, **29**, 96-100.

MARTINS, I.P., CASTRO-CALDAS, A., VAN DONGEN, H.R. and VAN HOUT, A. (eds) (1991). *Acquired Aphasia in Children: Acquisition and Breakdown of Language in the Developing Brain*. Dordrecht: Kluwer Academic Publications (in cooperation with NATO Scientific Affairs Division).

METTER, E.J. (1987). Neuroanatomy and physiology of aphasia: evidence from positron emission tomography. *Aphasiology*, **1**, 3-33.

MIDDLETON, J. (1989). Annotation: Thinking about head injuries in children. *Journal of Child Psychology and Psychiatry*, **30**, 663-670.

MORRELL, F., WHISLER, W.W. and BLECK, T.P. (1989). Multiple subpial transection: A new approach to the surgical treatment of focal epilepsy. *Journal of Neurosurgery*, **70**, 231-239.

MURDOCH, B.E. (ed.) (1990). *Acquired Neurological Speech/Language Disorders in Childhood*. London: Taylor & Francis.

MURDOCH, B.E. and OZANNE, A.E. (1990). Linguistic status following acute cerebral anoxia in children. In: B.E. Murdoch (ed.), *Acquired Neurological Speech/Language Disorders in Childhood*. London: Taylor & Francis.

NEALE, M.D. (1958). *Neale Analysis of Reading Ability*. London: Macmillan.

NEWTON, A. and THOMPSON, M. (1976). *The Aston Index*. Wisbech: Learning Development Aids.

PAGET, R., GORMAN, P. and PAGET, G. (1976). *The Paget Gorman Sign System*. London: Association for Experiment in Deaf Education.

PAQUIER, P., SAERENS, J., PARIZEL, P.M. et al. (1989). Acquired reading disorder similar to pure alexia in a child with ruptured arteriovenous malformation. *Aphasiology*, **3**, 667-676.

PAQUIER, P. and VAN DONGEN, H.R. (1991). Two contrasting cases of fluent aphasia in children. *Aphasiology*, (3), 235-245.

PARMELEE, D.X. and O'SHANICK, G.J. (1987). Neuropsychiatric intervention with head injured children and adolescents. *Brain Injury*, **1**, 41-47.

PASSY, J. (1990). *Cued Articulation*. Australian Council for Educational Research. Available from ICAN, 10 Bowling Green Lane, London EC1R 0BD.

PENFIELD, W. and RASMUSSEN, T. (1950). *The Cerebral Cortex of Man*. London: Macmillan.

PORCH, B. (1972). *The Porch Index of Communicative Ability in Children*. Palo Alto: Consulting Psychologist Press.

RAPIN, I. and ALLEN, D.A. (1987). Developmental Dysphasia and Autism in Preschool Children: Characteristics and Subtypes. Proceedings of 1st Symposium on Speech and Language Disorders in Children, Reading, UK. London: AFASIC.

RENFREW, C. (1977a, 1989). *The Word Finding Vocabulary Test*. Published by the author at North Place, Old Headington, Oxford, UK.

RENFREW, C. (1977b). *The Bus Story Test*. Published by the author at North Place, Old Headington, Oxford, UK.

RENFREW, C. (1988). *The Action Picture Test*. Published by the author at North Place, Old Headington, Oxford, UK.

RETT, A. (1966). *Uber ein Zerebral-atrophisches Syndrom bei Hyperammonamie.* Wein: Bruder Hollinek

RETT, A. (1969). Hyperammonaemie und cerebrale atrophie im kindesalter. *Folia Hereditaria et Pathologica,* **18**, 115-124.

REYNELL, J. (1985). *The Reynell Developmental Language Scales (revised)* Winsdor: NFER-Nelson.

RIPLEY, K. and LEA, J. (1984). *Moor House School: a follow up study of receptive aphasic ex-pupils.* Moor House School, Oxted, Surrey.

RIVA, D., PANTALEONI, C., MILANI, N. and DEVOTI, M. (1991). Late sequelae of right versus left hemispheric lesions. In: I.P. Martins, A. Castro-Caldas, H.R. Van Dongen and A. Van Hout (eds), *Acquired Aphasia in Children: Acquisition and Breakdown of Language in the Developing Brain.* Dordrecht: Kluwer Academic Publications (in cooperation with NATO Scientific Affairs Division).

ROBINSON, R.J. (1987). The causes of language disorder: introduction and overview. Proceedings of the First International Symposium of Specific Speech and Language Disorders in Children, Reading, England. London: AFASIC.

ROBINSON, R.J. (1991). Causes and association of severe and persistent specific speech and language disorders in children. *Developmental Medicine and Child Neurology,* **33**, 943-962.

ROBINSON, R.O. (1988). Investigations in children with acquired autism. Paper presented at 'Syndromes of Acquired Autism'; meeting of the Royal Society of Medicine, 13 December 1988, London.

ROBINSON, R.O. (1992). Brain imaging and language. In: P. Fletcher and D. Hall (eds), *Specific Speech and Language Disorders in Children.* London: Whurr Publishers.

ROSS, E.M., PECKHAM, C.S., WEST, P.R. and BUTLER, N.R. (1987). Epilepsy in childhood: findings from the National Child Development Study. *British Medical Journal,* **1**, 207-210.

RUTTER, M. (1978). Diagnosis and Definition. In: M. Rutter, and E. Schopler (eds), *Autism: A Reappraisal of Concepts and Treatment.* New York: Plenum Press.

SATZ, P. (1991). Symptom pattern and recovery outcome in childhood aphaisa: a methodological and theoretical critique. In: I.P. Martins, A. Castro-Caldas, H.R. Van Dongen and A. Van Hout (eds), *Acquired Aphasia in Children: Acquisition and Breakdown of Language in the Developing Brain.* Dordrecht: Kluwer Academic Publications (in cooperation with NATO Scientific Affairs Division).

SMITH, M.C., WHISLER, W.W. and MORRELL, F. (1989). Neurosurgery of epilepsy. *Seminars in Neurology,* **9**, 231-247.

SMITH, T. (1991). *Communicating Quality: Professional Standards for Speech and Language Therapists.* London: The College of Speech and Language Therapists.

SMYTH, V., OZANNE, A.E. and WOODHOUSE, L.M. (1990). Communicative Disorders in Childhood Infectious Diseases. In: B.E. Murdoch (ed.), *Acquired Neurological Speech/Language Disorders in Childhood.* London: Taylor & Francis.

SPREEN, O. and BENTON, A.L. (1969). *Neurosensory Centre Comprehensive Examination for Aphasia.* Australia: University of Victoria.

VAN DER SANDT-KOENDERMAN, W.M.E., SMIT, I.A.C., VAN DONGEN, H.R. and VAN HEST, J.B.C. (1984). A case of acquired aphasia with convulsive disorder; some linguistic aspects of recovery and breakdown. *Brain and Language,* **21**, 174-183.

VAN DONGEN, H.R. and LOONEN, M.C.B. (1977). Factors related to prognosis of acquired aphasia in children. *Cortex,* **13**, 131-136.

VAN DONGEN, H.R. and PAQUIER, P. (1991). Fluent aphasias in children. In: I.P. Martins, A. Castro-Caldas, Van Dongen, H.R. and A. Van Hout (eds), *Acquired Aphasia in*

Children: Acquisition and Breakdown of Language in the Developing Brain. Dordrecht: Kluwer Academic Publications (in cooperation with NATO Scientific Affairs Division).

VAN DONGEN, H.R. and VISCH-BRINK, E.G. (1988). Naming in aphasic children: analysis of paraphasic errors. *Neuropsychologia*, **26**, 629–632.

VAN DONGEN, H.R., LOONEN, M.C.B. and VAN DONGEN, K.J. (1985) Anatomical basis for acquired fluent aphasia in children. *Annals of Neurology*, **17**, 306–309.

VAN DONGEN, H., MEULSTEE, J., BLAUW-VAN-MOURIK, M. and VAN HARSKAMP, F. (1989). Landau–Kleffner Syndrome: A case study with a fourteen year follow-up. *European Neurology*, **29**, 109–114.

VAN HARSKAMP, F., VAN DONGEN H.R. and LOONEN, M.C.B. (1978). Acquired aphasia with convulsive disorder in children; a case study with a seven year follow up. *Brain and Language*, **6**, 141–148.

VAN HOUT, A. (1991). Outcome of acquired aphasia in childhood: Prognostic factors. In: I.P. Martins, A. Castro-Caldas, H.R. Van Dongen and A. Van Hout (eds), *Acquired Aphasia in Children: Acquisition and Breakdown of Language in the Developing Brain*. Dordrecht: Kluwer Academic Publications (in cooperation with NATO Scientific Affairs Division).

VAN HOUT, A., EVRARD, P. and LYON, G. (1985). On the positive semiology of acquired aphasia in children. *Developmental Medicine and Child Neurology*, **27**, 231–241.

VANCE, M. (1991). Educational and therapeutic approaches used with a child with acquired aphasia with convulsive disorder (Landau–Kleffner Syndrome). *Child Language, Teaching and Therapy*, **7**, 41–60.

VARGHA-KHADEM, F., O'GORMAN, A.M. and WATTERS, G.V. (1985). Aphasia and handedness in relation to hemispheric side, age at injury and severity of cerebral lesions during childhood. *Brain*, **108**, 677–696.

VERNON, P.E. (1977). *Graded Word Spelling Test*. London: Hodder & Stoughton.

VOLKMAR, F.R. and COHEN, D.J. (1989). Disintegrative disorder or 'Late Onset Autism'. *Journal of Child Psychology and Psychiatry*, **30**, 717–724.

WALKER, M. (1980). *The Revised Makaton Vocabulary*. Published by the author at St Georges' Hospital, London.

WARD, J.D. and ALBERICO, A.M. (1987). Paediatric head injuries. *Brain Injury*, **1**, 21–25.

WECHSLER, D. (1974). *Wechsler Intelligence Scale for Children (revised)*. New York: Psychological Corporation.

WHURR, R. (1974). *An Aphasia Screening Test*. Published by the author at the National Hospital for Nervous Diseases, London.

WHURR, R. and EVANS, S. (1986). *The Children's Aphasia Screening Test*. London: Whurr Publishers.

WHURR, R., LORCH, M.P. and NYE, C. (1992). A meta-analysis of studies carried out between 1946 and 1988 concerned with the efficacy of speech and language therapy treatment for aphasic patients. *European Journal of Disorders of Communication*, **27**, 1–18.

WOODS, B.T. and TEUBER, H.L. (1978). Changing patterns in childhood aphasia. *Annals of Neurology*, **3**, 273–280.

WORSTER-DROUGHT, C. (1956). Congenital suprabulbar paresis. *Journal of Layngology and Otology*, **70**, 453–463.

WORSTER-DROUGHT, C. (1971). An unusual form of acquired aphasia in children. *Developmental Medicine and Child Neurology*, **13**, 563–571.

YLVISAKER, M. (1985). *Head Injury Rehabilitation: Children and Adolescents*. London: Taylor & Francis.

Index